I0459770

SOBER WITCH LIFE

A Magickal Guide to Recovery

Sunshine Witchski

Illuminate: The Unschool of Sober Witchcraft

ISBN: 979-8-9920943-0-5

Published by Illuminate: The Unschool of Sober Witchcraft
First Edition

For inquiries or permissions, contact:
headmistress@illuminateunschool.com

——-

——-

Disclaimer: The information in this book is intended to provide helpful and informative material on the subjects discussed.
It is not meant to replace professional medical or therapeutic advice. The reader should consult a licensed professional for any mental health, medical, or recovery-related concerns.

*This book is dedicated to those that we lost to addiction.
May your souls rest easy and watch over us from above.*

"We do not find magick outside of ourselves; we awaken to the magick that has always been within."

UNKNOWN

"I wholeheartedly recommend Sober Witch Life: A Magickal Guide to Recovery to anyone considering recovery or already on their journey—especially those who are also drawn to witchcraft. This book is compassionate, insightful, and packed with actionable steps—no filler. Sunshine Witchski generously shares her own experience, demonstrating that she has truly walked this path, while always keeping the focus on empowering the reader.

She thoughtfully reinterprets the traditional 12-step program, transforming it into an embodied Magickal practice that feels both accessible and deeply transformative. The book is brilliantly structured, offering unique and engaging meditations, visualizations, mantras, spells, and rituals. While Sunshine acknowledges the challenges of sobriety, she provides so much meaningful, hands-on work that the process becomes not only uplifting but enjoyable. She even includes exquisitely inventive mocktails—or rather, Magicktails!

Take your time with this creative, healing book. You will be inspired."

— Amanda R. Howland
Yoga teacher | Author of the novels Mona Cost Returns to the Black House and Beasts and Creature
amandarhowland.com

"Working with Sunshine is nothing short of transformational. She has created a space of deep healing, sustainable recovery, and unwavering support—a sanctuary where growth is constant and perspectives are ever-expanding. Through the Witch's 13 Steps to Recovery, she has woven a path that blends Magick, accountability, and radical self-empowerment, offering a truly holistic approach to sobriety.

From the moment I stepped into this journey with her, I felt seen, understood, and profoundly guided. This is not just recovery—it's a reclamation of personal power, a return to Magick, and a rebirth into a life of true alignment. The Sober Witch Life: A Magickal Road to Recovery isn't just a book; it's a living, breathing roadmap to a life filled with purpose, clarity, and connection. I am endlessly grateful for the wisdom and light Sunshine brings, and I look forward to continuing this sacred work alongside her."

— Kimberly Vomero
Registered Clinical Social Work Intern, MSW | Recovery Ally

"Sunshine's fierce passion and dedication to supporting witches in recovery is palpable in every offering she creates—including this book. Her deep compassion and commitment to service come directly from her own lived experience, from battling addiction to using her intuitive gifts and innate Magick to break free in the most powerful way.

I have gained so much from working with her in Illuminate to strengthen my own intuitive abilities—I can't even put it into words! Trust me when I say this book, along with all the Magick and resources inside, will revolutionize your recovery journey. And while you're at it, join us in the Recovery Coven—it's the spiritual family you never knew you needed!"

— Ruby Hernandez
LMFT, E-RYT | Sound Healer | Recovery Ally
www.HolisticTherapyLMFT.com

"I've been part of Sunshine's Sober Witch programming since its inception, and it has been an absolute gift on my recovery journey. The sense of community is unparalleled—being surrounded by witches who truly understand my struggles has been profoundly healing. Sober Witch Life and The Witch's 13 Steps to Recovery have been invaluable as I navigate my addiction to dopamine, offering guidance, support, and Magickal alignment exactly when I need it most."

— Heather Powers
Creative Spirituality Mentor | Intuitive Healer | Soul Song Alchemist
www.soulsongalchemy.net

"Sunshine's integration of spirituality with recovery allows readers to experience the profound healing power of transforming addiction into a catalyst for self-understanding, self-love, and reclamation."

— Graham Skidmore
Founder, EnGen – A Non-Profit for Personal Empowerment
www.engensolutions.com

PREFACE

This book was written over the course of my first five years of sobriety, with much of the initial draft completed in my second year. Writing it has been an incredibly healing journey for me—one that has unfolded like a ritual of self-discovery, transformation, and magick.

As I edited, new memories surfaced, some gentle, others raw, reminding me of the pivotal moments that shaped my recovery. I was pulled back into the dark corners I once inhabited, but also into the glimmers of hope that guided me forward. Each chapter became a spell of remembrance, a testimony to the power of resilience, and a whispered invocation to the witches who, like me, are navigating sobriety with spirit and fire.

This book is more than just a collection of words—it's a talisman. A sacred offering. A guide meant to illuminate your own path through the shadows and into your power. My hope is that as you move through these pages, you find not just reflections of your own experiences, but also the tools, wisdom, and magick to make your recovery uniquely yours.

INTRODUCTION

You will find many journal prompts throughout the book, along with exercises and Magickal work designed to guide your recovery. I strongly suggest having a notebook at hand, along with some highlighters and those little paper flags to mark important parts. This book is not meant to sit passively on a shelf; it's meant to be used, written in, and revisited. Put it to work, and let it guide you through your recovery as a witch.

Here's a best practice: read through the book once to get a sense of the journey, and then come back to work through each chapter individually. Alternatively, you may choose to go one chapter at a time from the start, focusing deeply on each aspect of your recovery. There's no right or wrong way—follow what feels best for your path.

If you're feeling uncertain about where to begin, skip ahead to Chapter 14 and work through the foundational pieces. That chapter will help you get grounded and provide the clarity you need to begin at Step One. Remember, you are never alone on this journey; the Magick within you and my support are here to guide you.

PROLOGUE

Our ancestors are the echoes of wisdom in our blood, guiding us with unseen hands and whispering ancient truths to light our path when we feel lost.

This book is only one step among many on my journey through a spiritual path that has been long and bumpy. It has wound through various relationships, hardships, jobs, a marriage, a divorce, and ultimately, the realization that I am an alcoholic. So, let's face it—this book isn't just for you. It's also for me. As I write this prologue, I am 15 months into my recovery. If there's one thing I've learned through this journey, it's that we must constantly revisit why we are doing this, what brought us to the decision to become sober, and why we continue down this path.

It's not just a conversation with ourselves; it's a conversation with those around us. I offer this book to all of you as another way to help me stay sober. Thank you for that opportunity.

As the 12th step says, once we've had a spiritual awakening, we must share that message with others to continue our recovery. About a month and a half into my own sober journey, I had an epiphany about how deeply sobriety had already shaped my life—something I hadn't realized before. Before we embark on this 13-step journey together, I want to introduce you to my grandfather, Hugh Babb.

I won't claim to know the exact story, as I wasn't there, but I'll share what I remember. These stories are a blend of those passed down to me and ones I've uncovered as I embraced my mediumship abilities. And let me tell you, these stories impacted me profoundly during the early days of my recovery.

One day, sitting at an AA meeting, my spirit guides flashed a memory of my grandfather before me. Although I never saw him drink, I knew he was an alcoholic. My mind wandered to the story I'd heard about how he met my grandmother...

When my grandfather first met my grandmother, she already had eight children ranging from toddlers to young adults. The eldest son, my uncle, found himself in trouble, and a stranger —my grandfather—cared enough to step in. Seeing what a loving and compassionate man my grandfather was, someone suggested that he help my uncle clean up his act. My grandfather showed up at my grandmother's door with my uncle (who, to be fair, was a bit of a delinquent) to express his concern and offer his help.

I'm not entirely sure how he courted my grandmother, and while I could connect with him on the other side to find out, what struck me at that AA table was this: the 12th step is what brought my grandfather into our family's life.

From that moment, my bond with my grandfather transformed and deepened. He became one of my spirit guides, someone I call upon when I need extra help in my sobriety. He's also the guide I ask to watch over others struggling with addiction. And so, as I write these words, I invite you to ask your ancestors for guidance and comfort along your own journey.

Blessed Be my dear witches.

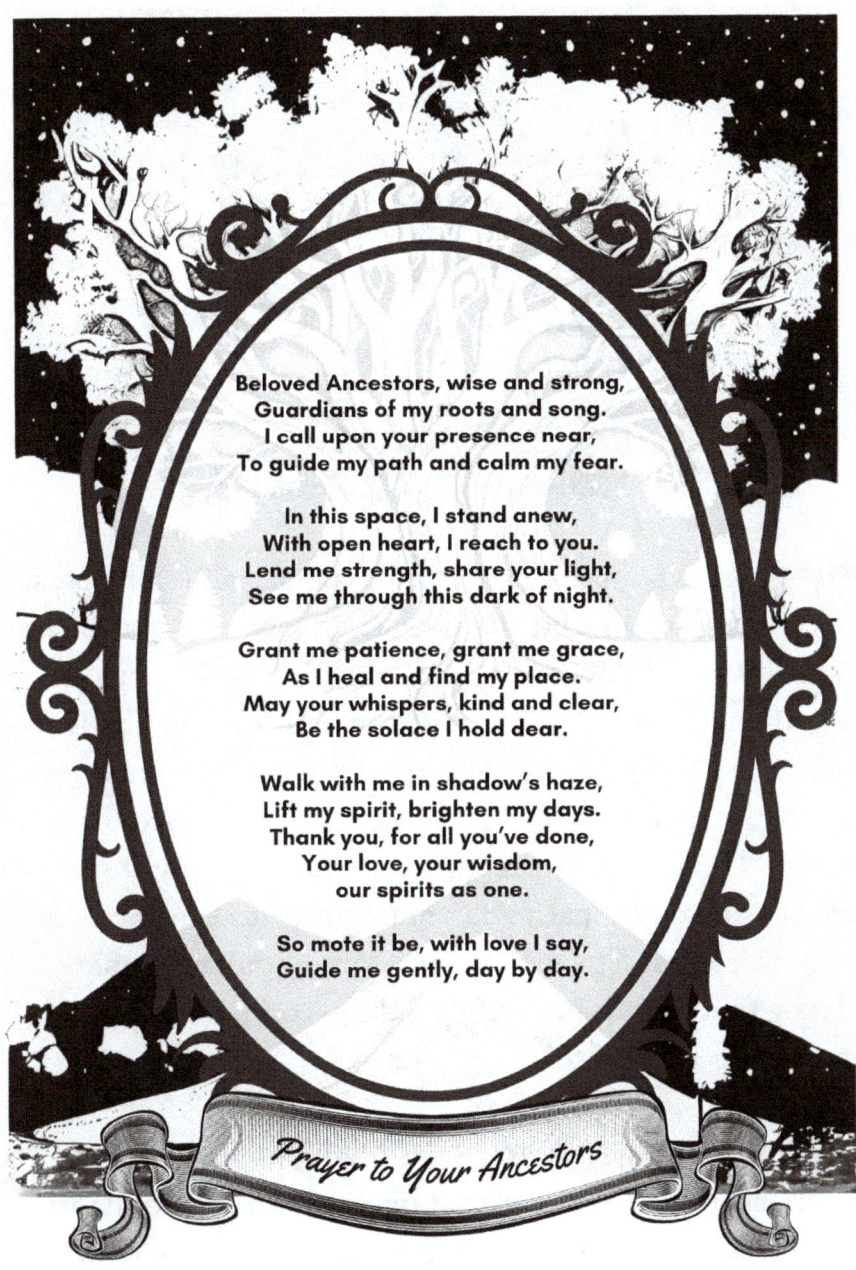

Beloved Ancestors, wise and strong,
Guardians of my roots and song.
I call upon your presence near,
To guide my path and calm my fear.

In this space, I stand anew,
With open heart, I reach to you.
Lend me strength, share your light,
See me through this dark of night.

Grant me patience, grant me grace,
As I heal and find my place.
May your whispers, kind and clear,
Be the solace I hold dear.

Walk with me in shadow's haze,
Lift my spirit, brighten my days.
Thank you, for all you've done,
Your love, your wisdom,
our spirits as one.

So mote it be, with love I say,
Guide me gently, day by day.

Prayer to Your Ancestors

The Witch's 13 Steps To Recovery

Throughout the course of this book, I will share personal reflections and insights from my own journey as a witch in recovery. Each chapter will focus on one step, diving deeper into its meaning and guiding you through working it for yourself. But before we begin that journey together, it felt essential to present these 13 steps in their entirety. This way, you can pause, reflect, and truly absorb what this transformative path will entail. Embrace this moment and the power these steps hold—you are about to embark on a journey that invites profound healing, connection, and Magick into your recovery.

1. **Embrace Powerlessness, Seek Change** – I accept that I am powerless over alcohol and that my life has become chaotic and difficult because of it. This acceptance opens the doorway to transformation, where surrender becomes a powerful first act of Magick in my recovery.

2. Trust in Divine Guidance – I believe that a force greater than myself can lift me from the shadows, guiding me toward higher vibrations and a life illuminated by healing light. This power is my connection to the divine, ancestors, or spirit guides who stand by me.

3. Align with Universal Flow – I choose to embrace my psychic gifts and allow the Universe to direct my spiritual path without my interference. This alignment invites synchronicity and the flow of Magick into every moment of my recovery journey.

4. Engage in Shadow Work – I commit to deep, honest shadow work, uncovering hidden aspects of myself that need healing. I seek out the buried wounds, bringing light to them with courage and rituals of release, allowing growth to flourish.

5. Release Burdens with Community – I recognize that I cannot carry the weight of my past alone. Through authentic connection and belonging, I release guilt and find solace in the shared energy of my coven and allies.

6. Invoke Magick for Liberation – I am ready to call upon my inner and outer Magick to release the past, stepping forward into my life's highest purpose. I do this by weaving rituals and intentions that empower me to vibrate in alignment with my truth.

7. Craft Daily Rituals for Blessings – I infuse my daily life with Magickal practices that attract positive energy and health.

These rituals serve as touchstones, blessing me with protection, vitality, and a strengthened will.

8. Make Amends with Sacred Lists – I create a comprehensive list of those I have wronged, including people, places, and energies, preparing to make heartfelt amends. This list is my map of reparations, leading me toward restorative balance.

9. Offer Intentional Spellwork for Healing – I take action by crafting intentional spellwork on behalf of those affected by my past actions, sending healing energy that mends the threads of our shared stories.

10. Sustain Growth with Ongoing Shadow Work – I continue to explore and heal whatever troubles arise, embracing shadow work as a lifelong practice. Through this, I find strength and a renewed sense of purpose, using my experiences to serve and uplift the world.

11. Connect with Guides for Clarity – I regularly meditate and reach out to my guides, ancestors, or deities for insight and direction. Their wisdom helps illuminate my path, ensuring I walk in harmony with my purpose and my spiritual mission.

12. Celebrate and Support Others – I honor each milestone, using my progress to deepen my witchcraft and evolve as a witch in recovery. I extend this energy outward by supporting and guiding other witches on their own journeys toward healing.

13. Rituals for Universal Release – I engage in spellwork and rituals that send energy to heal the collective, releasing the universe from the pain and suffering brought by addiction. Through sharing my story and contributing my Magick, I become a beacon of hope and transformation.

These are your steps, my dear witch—uniquely yours. And remember, you are not meant to walk this path alone. Recovery is a journey that thrives on connection, support, and shared strength. By opening this book, you have invited me to walk with you, and for that, I am deeply honored and grateful. Let this be a grounding moment, a sacred space where you take a deep breath and acknowledge that you are part of a greater circle of witches in recovery. Together, we will journey through these 13 steps, embracing Magick, community, and the resilience within.

CHAPTER ONE: MY ROCK BOTTOM

Your rock bottom is not the end; it's the solid foundation on which you rebuild your life.

I didn't go to sleep and wake up an alcoholic the next morning. As a matter of fact, you don't always notice the slow spiral because our inner "mind demon" can make everything appear perfect, distracting us from the chaos inside. We might find ourselves paying bills, achieving some goals, and living day-to-day life with fleeting moments of happiness. We might even be applauded for holding it all together.

For years, I convinced myself that my drinking wasn't a problem. But looking back now, I see the roots of that problem started when I was young. My first memory of seeking a drink was at the age of 8. I vividly remember the thrill when I found a half-finished drink my father had left on the end table. I didn't drink the whole thing but eagerly anticipated finding the next one. I liked the taste, but more than that, I craved the warm buzz that rolled over my tongue, down my throat, and seeped into my body.

My relationship with alcohol began then, and if I'm honest, it was always problematic. I remember sneaking sips from my dad's stash, figuring out which friends had parents with a well-stocked bar, and carefully measuring how much water to add back so no one would notice what I'd taken—all at just 11 years old. Admitting that out loud is hard. No, screw that—it's gut-wrenching to admit that my journey to rock bottom began so early.

Sitting at many recovery tables has taught me that my story isn't unique. If this resonates with you, know you're not alone. We all started somewhere, and we each have the choice to end the cycle.

Nearly 30 years of drinking led me to a swift, brutal decline. The blackouts came more often—you know, those nights you can't remember finishing your drink, waking up only to piece things together from the aftermath of a monstrous hangover or shame-filled texts. Then there were the flashbacks of raw anger that still smoldered in my chest the morning after.

Getting sober took me over a year and a half. I had been seeing a therapist for years, and in 2018, I finally began talking about my drinking as a potential problem. The idea of not drinking started to seem possible but distant, as if it were just a challenge to prove I could manage. I'd tell myself and others, **I could stop anytime —I'm strong enough to moderate**.

In January 2019, I committed to 90 days alcohol-free. It felt strange. I found myself in social situations fumbling for reasons why I wasn't ordering another round or savoring my go-to beer (Oh, Hopslam…). It was during these moments that subtle shifts began. I started asking myself why I drank and questioning the benefits. I even asked others why they drank, but none of their answers satisfied me.

Around day 83 of my 90-day journey, depression hit me like a storm I couldn't explain. The dark thoughts overwhelmed me, and in that moment, my 'drinking demon' claimed victory.

Seven days before the end of my challenge, I convinced myself that the only way out of this darkness was to drink. Drinking had always brought a fleeting sense of happiness, and I didn't want to feel that suffocating void any longer. So, I drank. What started as occasional drinks turned into daily binges over four months. I kept seeing my therapist, rationalizing every choice, convincing myself it wasn't a big deal.

July came, and my boyfriend and I were on vacation when he got sick. We had to cut our trip short and go home, and I was seething with rage.

How dare he get sick.

How dare he ruin my vacation.

How dare he make me drink alone on my time off.

The drinking continued. After a 10-day binge, I sat at my desk one Monday morning with a pounding head, drenched in cold sweat, slightly shaking. Tears welled up as I realized I was withdrawing from alcohol. Memories of that week—my anger, my selfishness—overwhelmed me with shame.

I had a therapy session that night. Through tears, I finally admitted, **I'm an alcoholic**.

I wish I could tell you that this was my rock bottom—that this moment snapped me into sobriety. But it wasn't. I knew I couldn't control alcohol, that it unleashed a side of me I hated, but that realization wasn't enough.

My true rock bottom came on my 40th birthday during a trip to Costa Rica. I had 63 days of sobriety under my belt but no tools to help me stay sober. Anxiety crashed over me as I watched my boyfriend buy his favorite bottle at the duty-free store. We hadn't discussed alcohol and vacations, so I tried to stay strong.

I lasted about three hours. At the swim-up bar, when he casually said, **I won't judge you if you drink**, I caved.

The rest of the week was a blur. On my birthday, we started drinking at 11 a.m., and by 5 p.m., we were drunk in the pool with strangers. Celebrating, right? But I'm an alcoholic. Alcohol holds power over me, and it brings chaos. The fight we had that night was so horrific that the resort gave him a separate room, free of charge. I became a person I don't even recognize—truly vicious.

There are photos of a special dinner that night, but I have no memory of it. I stayed up most of the night crying and talking to a friend, recording videos to remember it.

Remembering our rock bottom is essential for staying sober.

Even though I watched alcohol destroy my father and claim the life of my younger cousin, and despite admitting to my therapist that I was an alcoholic months before, it was my 40th birthday that anchored my decision to never touch alcohol again.

I share this so you know you're not alone. We each have our own rock bottom. Yours brought you to this book, and it matters. Embracing your story, accepting it as part of your journey, frees you to move forward.

Don't compare your story to mine. Every rock bottom is different, and yes, sometimes we hit it more than once. That's okay. This is a journey. I encourage you now to pause, reflect on your rock bottom, and give yourself a damn hug—you're taking the first step toward recovery.

And I'm honored to be part of it.

* * *

Journal Prompt:

Describe your rock bottom in detail. What did it feel like? Who was involved? What emotions dominated? Was it your first rock bottom? How was your life unmanageable? Was it reflected in your emotions, the situations around you, or those you created? Did it involve legal trouble? Financial trouble? Relationship trouble? Record your story in any form that resonates with you—writing, drawing, sketching, or even creating a video.

Remembering why we are on this path of recovery is an essential part of your transformational journey.

CHAPTER TWO: I NEED HELP AND I FUCKING NEED IT NOW

In the moment I admitted I couldn't do it alone, I found the strength to build a life rooted in truth and power.

At this point, I realized and had to accept that I couldn't do this alone. I had tried—and failed miserably. My boyfriend at the time, Keith, was himself a recovering addict. After a particularly intense last night in Costa Rica, he gave me an ultimatum. Deep down, I knew that, despite the harshness of his words, I was blessed to have someone who cared enough to push me. He told me that the only way we would stay together was if I promised and committed to doing 90 AA meetings in 90 days. That sounded fucking daunting.

I worked full-time, was heavily involved in a non-profit, and kept myself ridiculously busy. I thrived on filling my schedule to the brim, using busyness as a shield to hide from my own mess. Ninety meetings in 90 days? **How the fuck was I supposed to do that? Where would I even start? How would I find a meeting?** And did I really have to sit in front of a room full of strangers and share my story? My mind was a foggy haze from a recent binge, making it even harder to process what lay ahead.

We came back home, and there was an unmistakable shift between us. Silence filled spaces that were once lively, and the weight of my shame was suffocating. I was drowning in shame and guilt, each wave pulling me deeper. The cycle was repeating itself, and I knew it. The way I had treated Keith horrified me, especially after he finally reached out to his family—really opened up for the first time in years—to talk about what I had done. Sure, he had spoken to them before, but it was always superficial: a quick **Hi, how are you?** This time was different. He was honest, and I was at the center of it all. The guilt gnawed at me, an insidious reminder of how I could hurt those I loved when my addiction took control.

Desperate, I reached out to the only person I knew who had experience with AA. I met him when I was a teenager, and we used to work together in a retirement community working in their food service department. Outside of Facebook comments, we hadn't spoken since I was 17. Vulnerable and desperate, I messaged him, admitting that I had a problem and asking him to take me to a meeting. He had over a year in recovery at that point, and although he wasn't attending meetings regularly, he didn't hesitate. There was a kindness in his response that I hadn't expected, a reminder that people in recovery often hold an unspoken understanding of each other's silent battles. We met at a meeting near my house.

Walking into that room filled with strangers, I felt like I was stepping into a spotlight on the darkest stage of my life. My body was rigid, my hands clenched, and I sat at a table, tears streaming down my face. The mix of fear and vulnerability was unlike anything I'd ever felt. But thankfully, I didn't have to speak—I could just listen. The first realization that hit me was that there were others like me. They knew the relentless, gnawing grip of addiction. They knew the numbing cycles and the lies told to ourselves to make it okay.

I learned that when you're new to AA, meetings often focus on the first step. So, I sat and absorbed every word as each person at that table shared their rock bottom, their path to AA, and how they came to recognize that they were powerless over alcohol and that their lives had become unmanageable. Some stories mirrored mine—nights lost to the blur of alcohol, regret waking beside me in the morning like an unwanted companion. Others were even more harrowing, serving as both a warning and a source of solace.

Their stories mirrored my own, and for the first time, I felt less alone. I listened as they talked about finding a higher power, and it stirred something deep within me. Memories of my Catholic upbringing flooded back. I had attended Catholic school my entire childhood, experiencing uniforms that never fit right to nuns who scolded with looks that could pierce steel. But by my early teens, I began questioning it. The teachings started to feel more like chains than a path to understanding. By high school, I had fully accepted that I wasn't Catholic. The spirituality I craved aligned more with the path of a witch, and that realization had been fucking liberating.

But sitting at that AA table triggered a whirlwind of emotions connected to my spiritual journey. The term higher power hung in the air, stirring a mix of curiosity and defiance. I knew their God wasn't mine. But I also knew they were onto something crucial. I needed to rediscover my own spiritual path—one rooted in the Magick I had embraced as a teenager. It wasn't just about finding an external force to lean on; it was about reclaiming the parts of myself I'd buried under years of coping mechanisms.

So, I returned to my practice, this time with deeper intent. My higher power wasn't just one being or entity—it was everything. It was the universe, the spirit around me, the gods and goddesses, and every ancestor who had passed before me. It was no longer just my higher power; it was my higher powers. I needed this connection not only to stay sober but to rebuild who I was and who I wanted to be.

Journal Prompt

Take some time now to explore who, what, and where your higher power or powers are. Use a journal, sketch, or any creative outlet that resonates with you. Don't limit yourself—your higher power could be anything from a deity to an ancestor who struggled as you do, or even the universe itself. Some people find their higher power in nature or in science. Or maybe you do have a religion you're comfortable embracing, that's good too! The key is to make a choice, as this will be vital when you reach Step 3.

CHAPTER THREE: MY HIGHER POWERS TO THE RESCUE

Within us is the power to rise above our struggles, guided by the whispers of the unseen and the strength of our spirit.

At this stage, I was certain I'd found my higher powers. You should have seen the look on people's faces when I referred to them as my higher powers during meetings. There was always a mix of raised eyebrows and nods of understanding, a silent acknowledgment that we all had our own unique sources of strength. I was fortunate to be part of a community diverse in both religion and culture. Even though I wasn't sure everyone could relate to my path, I felt respected, and that made all the difference. This respect was vital, especially in those first few months that were marked by emotional upheavals I couldn't always control. It was like trying to ride a wild storm, never knowing when a wave would come crashing down or when I'd find a moment of stillness.

I oscillated between moments of complete chaos and brief flashes of lucidity. In hindsight, I realize the chaos stemmed from my relentless need to control my journey. I'd been clinging so tightly to the illusion of control that it consumed me. I was cautious to a fault, worrying endlessly about the future—how would I navigate the holidays? **What if I faltered in moments of vulnerability?** Each night, I went to meetings, baring my soul, and shared my swirling mix of fear, shame, and guilt. It was almost as if I were reliving my pain each time, hoping that somehow, speaking it out loud would break its hold over me. It took about a month before I could recount how I ended up at AA without tears streaming down my face.

Around the same time, my therapist and I started dissecting my long, complicated relationship with alcohol. And of course, you can't unpack that without bringing up my father, who struggled with alcoholism, or my mother, who was fiercely codependent. This exploration forced me to confront memories I had buried deep—a childhood marked by tension, the silence that echoed louder than words, and the subtle but constant reminder that things could unravel at any moment. These reflections were painful, but they were necessary for me to understand how deeply rooted my relationship with alcohol was.

A side note: AA also introduced me to Al-Anon, a group for those whose lives are impacted by alcoholics or addicts. Al-Anon was a revelation; it was like a secret door to a room full of people who understood the nuanced pain of loving an addict. It didn't matter if I was at an AA or an Al-Anon meeting—

everyone kept repeating the same advice: **Get a sponsor**. I tried. I spoke one-on-one with some wonderfully sober women, women who had years of experience navigating recovery and their own set of higher powers. But despite my efforts, nothing clicked. It wasn't me, and it wasn't them—it was simply a matter of timing and availability. The women I approached were already stretched thin, unable to commit to sponsoring someone new, and I respected that. Yet, it left a gap, a sense of uncertainty that gnawed at me.

Still, it made me wonder. About two months in, I sat in yet another meeting, feeling a strange mix of hope and frustration, reflecting on these conversations and the inspiring, spiritual women I'd met. It dawned on me that it had been a long time since I felt truly spiritually connected. This realization came with a wave of both sadness and determination. I needed something that went beyond the routine of meetings and check-ins. So, I picked up my tarot cards again, starting with simple readings for myself. The moment I held them, I was hit with a vivid memory of people at meetings mentioning the Third Step Prayer. Although I didn't have a sponsor to guide me through the steps, I knew deep down that I was ready to take this leap, to blend the traditional recovery path with the mystical practices that resonated with my soul.

So, I wrote my own Third Step Prayer. I've said some version of this prayer nearly every morning since. It was my way of blending the wisdom I'd gathered from AA with the practices that felt authentic to my spirit. It became a ritual, not just a prayer, infused with intention and connection to my higher powers.

God and goddesses, grandma, grandpa, Busha, Ja-Ja, Portia, Craig, and all the spirits and ancestors that surround me and protect me: Thank you for keeping me sober another day. For today, please take over and guide me down the right path to make the right decisions for me on this journey. Help me not pick up a drink.

In those early days, I didn't fully grasp just how transformative this practice would become. This simple prayer was more than a plea for guidance—it was an awakening, a reconnection to the psychic abilities that had been swirling within me for years. I was no longer just asking for help; I was reclaiming a power I had almost forgotten I possessed. The act of praying each morning began to feel less like a ritual obligation and more like a sacred dialogue, a moment of alignment where I felt deeply heard by the universe.

I first picked up a set of tarot cards when I was 16. Yes, I bought them for myself, and no, they weren't cursed. In fact, I still use that very deck for client readings today. The cards were my first introduction to trusting the unseen, to believing that there was more to life than what I could see or explain. Back then, I started pulling cards for myself and friends, captivated by how the messages resonated, sometimes uncannily so. Over the years, as life twisted and turned, I would occasionally bring out the cards from their navy-blue velvet bag and be amazed by the insight they offered. They had been a quiet presence through various stages of my life—sometimes tucked away, sometimes a guiding force—but always there.

Leaning on my psychic abilities through daily card readings

became a cornerstone of my recovery, marking a stark difference from the practices often discussed in AA. While some people spoke about praying over decisions, no one openly mentioned using psychic tools or any form of divination. It was uncharted territory, and in embracing it, I felt both exhilarated and quietly rebellious. This was my way of intertwining my identity as a witch with my journey toward sobriety, reclaiming the pieces of myself that addiction had fragmented.

✳ ✳ ✳

Journal Prompt:

Write a ritual prayer that calls upon your higher powers—your spirit guides, ancestors, the Universe, a deity, or any spiritual being you choose. Include these three parts:

- *Gratitude*
- *Release of control*
- *A request to stay free from your addiction*

Ritual Break:

Come on now—what kind of witch's recovery book would this be without some spells and rituals? Choose how you'll integrate this ritual prayer into your daily life. I recommend saying it in the morning or before bed. It's your ritual, your choice—just like it was my prayer to create. This simple morning prayer evolved into a 15-minute ritual for me.

- **Step 1:** *Begin your day with your newly written Third Step Prayer.*
- **Step 2:** *Use your favorite divination tool—tarot cards, an oracle deck, your pendulum, divining rods, or runes.*
- **Step 3:** *Ask these questions:*
  - *Tarot/Oracle/Runes:*
    - *What is helping me stay on the path of recovery?*
    - *What might put my recovery at risk?*
  - *Pendulum/Divining Rods:*
    - *Am I on my highest vibrational path?*
    - *Have any of my actions put my recovery at risk?*
- **BONUS:** *Mix pendulum work with cards or runes for deeper insights.*

Note: Record these answers in a daily journal. This practice helps identify patterns and provides a point of reflection as you continue on your journey.

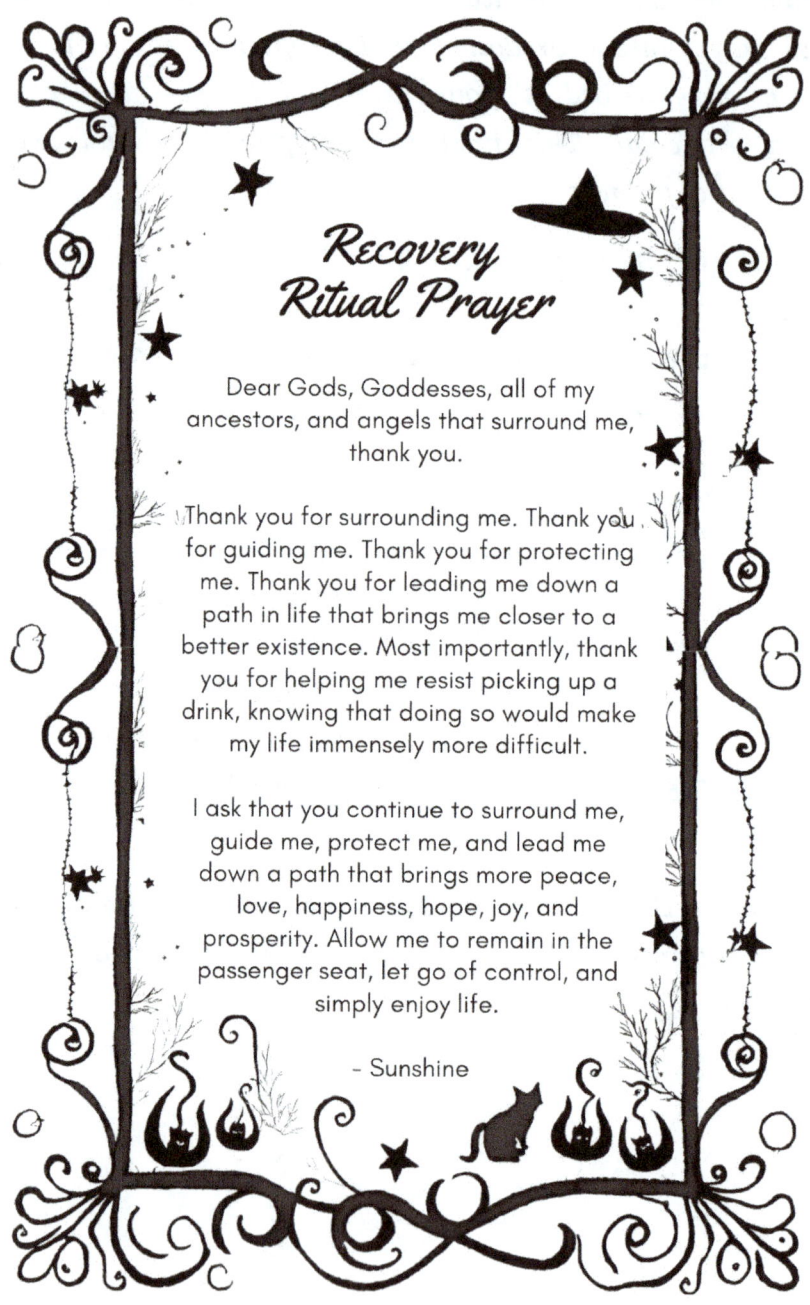

Recovery Ritual Prayer

Dear Gods, Goddesses, all of my ancestors, and angels that surround me, thank you.

Thank you for surrounding me. Thank you for guiding me. Thank you for protecting me. Thank you for leading me down a path in life that brings me closer to a better existence. Most importantly, thank you for helping me resist picking up a drink, knowing that doing so would make my life immensely more difficult.

I ask that you continue to surround me, guide me, protect me, and lead me down a path that brings more peace, love, happiness, hope, joy, and prosperity. Allow me to remain in the passenger seat, let go of control, and simply enjoy life.

- Sunshine

CHAPTER FOUR: DID SOMEBODY TURN OUT THE LIGHTS?

The shadows we confront are the keys to understanding the light within us. True growth comes not from avoiding our darkness, but from bravely facing it.

Not going to lie—I dreaded this step when I was sitting at the tables in AA. When you're there with so many others, you start to notice that this step is one that many people fear. But looking back, it's obvious why it's necessary. It's even more clear why it comes after Step 3, when we let go of control and allow our spirit guides, ancestors, or the universe to guide us. Because if we don't, what AA refers to as our inventory becomes an incredibly tough process.

Now, you might be asking, **what the fuck is an inventory?**

It's shadow work. That term most of us witches have heard but not everyone fully understands. Let me explain. Shadow work involves digging into the deep, dark parts of ourselves to uncover what we might have avoided facing. It's intended for profound, spiritual learning. You know you're doing shadow work right when it makes you deeply uncomfortable—when you find yourself sobbing, overwhelmed by intense feelings of shame, guilt, and remorse. And let me tell you, this exercise was one hell of an experience for me. It felt like ripping open old wounds, ones I didn't even know were still festering.

If you're interested, you can find worksheets online to guide you through it the AA way. But instead of detailing how I did it my first time, I'm going to share some of the things I discovered —the hard truths that slapped me in the face and changed everything.

My story isn't outwardly destructive. I've never been to jail. The only court cases I've been involved in were for a minor speeding ticket and my divorce. I've never lost a job over drinking. But when I looked closer, patterns started to emerge. I saw my controlling nature. I would never let myself be in a situation that could land me in jail. I made sure I was never in court for anything serious or seen as a criminal. And you bet I was always the number one employee at any job. Control—that was my pattern, my armor, my survival tactic. The more I controlled, the more I thought I could keep the chaos at bay.

My father was an alcoholic with a temper, so growing up, you had to tread carefully around him. Through my shadow work, I realized how much of my life I spent seeking his approval, trying to make him happy. Because if he was happy, he wouldn't get angry. And if he didn't get angry... well, if you've ever lived in a home with an angry alcoholic, you know the tension, the unspoken threat of what could happen next. That's where my deep, clawing fear of failure was born. It wasn't just a fear of making mistakes; it was a fear of what those mistakes could trigger.

I could also see my mother's co-dependency. It became glaringly obvious how she would go out of her way to please my father and even us kids, no matter how much it cost her emotionally or mentally. I never once saw her stand up for herself. This is where my fear of standing up for myself came from—an inheritance I didn't ask for but accepted without question.

I saw my relationship with my ex-husband for what it really was: a childhood crush built over cases of beer. Interestingly enough, as I write this now, I realize how much he mirrored my father. My dad was happiest after two drinks, and my ex-husband? I often told him he was way more fun after a couple of beers. I learned to tolerate addiction behavior, to look the other way, and even laugh it off as a quirk instead of recognizing it as a red flag.

I looked at my friendship with my ex-best friend and saw it for what it was—a co-dependent relationship where I was constantly taking care of her, regardless of how she treated me. Despite that gnawing feeling in my gut that screamed this wasn't right, I stayed. I ignored my intuition because it was easier to focus on someone else's problems than face my own. The painful realization was that this pattern wasn't about love or loyalty—it was about distraction and avoidance.

I saw how multiple romantic relationships failed because I was too afraid to be vulnerable or too controlling to allow any room for mistakes. I'd build walls and fortresses around myself, thinking that would keep me safe, but instead, it kept me trapped and disconnected. And lastly, I faced the truth of that little black book—filled with names, faces, and blank spaces that represented all the times I used sex to fill a deep-rooted desire for emotional intimacy. It was a void I tried to plaster over with superficial connections, hoping they would stick, but they never did.

It wasn't just about what I learned; it was about what I finally accepted. My life wasn't as great as I thought it was. For the first time, I understood why alcohol had taken such a firm hold on me. Instead of accepting these experiences as part of who I was and seeing the good they brought into my life, I chose to hide from them. I chose alcohol to numb myself, to buy into the twisted belief that partying was life's ultimate goal. It reinforced a warped view of success and made me believe that the emptiness was normal.

Now that I've shared some of my dirty secrets, it's your turn to get real. It's time to commit to deep, intense, honest Shadow work, just as this step asks of you. Remember, you don't have to do it alone or make it up as you go. I'm here to guide you through it.

How to Do Recovery Shadow Work

Working through these questions is essential for diving deep into the roots of your relationship with alcohol and understanding its impact on your life. Shadow work can be intense, unearthing emotions and memories that may feel overwhelming. That's why it's important to pace yourself— take on just a few questions at a time and give yourself space to process what comes up. The goal is to confront and accept these shadows, bit by bit, so that you can reclaim your power and move forward with clarity and strength. Approach this work with patience and kindness toward yourself; you're doing brave, transformative work.

Solo

You may often hear that you should work on this with someone. If you have someone you trust who has been through recovery themselves, then by all means, do so. If not, it's perfectly acceptable to use one of the methods outlined below.

Journaling

One of the most common forms of shadow work is journaling, using prompts to explore your thoughts and feelings. Honesty is key as you respond. If writing isn't your thing, consider video journaling. Be raw and truthful. Afterward, make sure you revisit your entries to reflect.

Early Life Prompts

- *When was the first time you remember engaging in the behavior?*

- *What did it feel like?*
- *When was the first time you remember seeking out a drink?*
- *What was the relationship with alcohol/vice around you as a child?*

Teenage Year Prompts

- *What kind of peer pressure was there to drink?*
- *Did you hang out with kids who drank, or did you avoid them?*
- *How did it feel when you chose not to drink or said no?*
- *Did you ever say no?*
- *What did people say about those who didn't drink?*
- *What were the people like who did drink?*

Work Prompts

- *Have you ever drunk at a work function? Hidden a drink?*
- *Have you ever drunk at work? What thoughts crossed your mind, and how did it make you feel?*
- *Have you shown up to work hungover? How did that impact your performance and feelings?*
- *Have you ever faced discipline while drunk or hungover? What emotions did that stir? How did you respond?*

Relationship Prompts

- *Who were the people you drank with?*
- *How did you react when someone said they didn't want to drink?*
- *How did you respond when someone wouldn't drink when you wanted them to?*
- *How many arguments have you had while drunk? How many did you regret the next day?*

- *How many arguments have you had while hungover, and did any linger beyond the day?*
- *Are you holding on to any arguments now? Who aren't you speaking to?*

Intimacy Prompts

- *How often do you have sex without alcohol?*
- *How often do intimate moments happen without alcohol?*
- *When was the last time you cried in front of someone? Who was it, and why?*
- *If you don't remember, why is that?*
- *Have you ever used alcohol to create intimacy? Why?*
- *Have you ever regretted sex? Was alcohol involved?*

Finance Prompts

- *How much money do you regularly spend on alcohol?*
- *Have you ever delayed paying a bill to afford alcohol?*
- *Do you pay your bills on time? Why or why not?*
- *Do you have savings? Why or why not?*
- *Have you made any regrettable purchases under the influence?*

Through Tarot Spreads

Tarot cards can be invaluable tools for insight, especially when memories blur after years of drinking. They offer a new lens to explore the role of alcohol in your life, beyond journaling. You can of course use all the same prompts above, but sometimes simple, to the point questions are easier to use when pulling cards so I've revised some of them for you to use below.

Of course, some of you may also be wondering, "Can I use Oracle cards instead?" Absolutely you can. I'd encourage you to use whatever divinatory method you are most comfortable with.

The Beginning Prompts

- *What was your initial relationship with alcohol like?*
- *What aspect of your life did alcohol impact the most when you began?*
- *What did you think alcohol provided you at first?*
- *Why did you pick up your first drink?*

Teenage Year Prompts

- *What was your main reason for drinking as a teen?*
- *What role did alcohol play in your teenage years?*
- *Why didn't you choose not to drink?*

Work Prompts

- *How did alcohol impact your career?*
- *How might your career evolve on your recovery journey?*
- *What lesson should you remember from your past work experience regarding alcohol?*

Relationship Prompts

- *How has your relationship with your parents changed?*
- *How about your siblings? Friends? Significant other?*
- *How would these relationships differ if addiction hadn't been present?*

Intimacy Prompts

- *How has alcohol affected your romantic life?*
- *What would intimacy look like without alcohol?*

- *How would your sexual relationships change in the absence of addiction?*

Finance Prompts

- *What's your current relationship with money?*
- *How would it change without addiction?*
- *What new perspective on money could you adopt?*
- *How could money support your recovery?*

With Others

If you choose to involve others in your recovery, the most important thing is ensuring that the people you work with have gone through their own recovery journey. YES, seeing a therapist can be incredibly beneficial, but they can't replace the insights and support you get from someone who's **been there, done that**.

Coach

Recovery coaches are a great option. These are usually people who have been through recovery programs themselves (ideally one that aligns with yours). If you need some extra accountability to stay sober, I highly recommend looking for a recovery coach. Here's what to keep in mind when finding the right one:

What to Look For in a Coach

- *They share an approach to recovery that speaks to you. For instance, some programs have strong Christian-based beliefs— if that's not your thing, keep looking.*

- *They offer a sliding scale for payment so cost isn't a barrier.*
- *They have referrals you can contact to vouch for their experience.*
- *They run their coaching like a professional business.*

What to Watch Out For in a Coach

- *While it may sound strict, I recommend working with someone where there is no potential for mutual attraction. Even experienced recovery individuals have their own challenges, and stories about 'sponsors' overstepping boundaries aren't unheard of. While these stories rarely involve coaches, many follow this guideline for safety.*
- *Coaches who don't have any referrals or avoid letting you speak with them directly before beginning to work with them. Excuses here can be a red flag.*

Should You Pay for Coaching?

A solid coach dedicates their time and expertise to help you. If you're serious about your recovery and want that extra layer of support, investing in a coach is worth it. If that's not feasible, look for free or donation-based support groups.

Group

And yes, this could mean attending an AA meeting. My local AA chapter has been open and welcoming to my spiritual beliefs. Sure, I may have gotten a few odd looks initially, but being in an area with diverse religions helped. If AA isn't an option for you (some areas are less witch-friendly), there are other ways to find support:

- **Facebook Groups:** *I run a Sober Witches group within my Facebook community, and you're welcome to join. There are other sober-focused groups that have supported me in tough times when I needed extra love or couldn't attend a local AA meeting.*

- **Local Meetups:** *Seek out witchy groups and be upfront about needing support for deep shadow work. You might find someone who's gone through recovery and can offer guidance. These spaces can become safe places to share your experiences and challenges. Remember, your story might encourage someone else to confront their own shadow.*

Note: Always vet the hosts of Facebook or Meetup groups to ensure their values align with yours.

Remember, shadow work is an ongoing practice. As witches, we know our shadows can creep back up if we don't continually acknowledge and accept them. If you ever find yourself tempted to drink or feeling weighed down by regret, shame, or anger, return to your shadow work. It's your guide, your reminder that you're not alone in this journey. Embrace the tools and community that resonate with you, and know that every step forward is a testament to your resilience and Magickal power. You've got this.

CHAPTER FIVE: STEPPING INTO THE LIGHT

*"Vulnerability sounds like truth and feels like courage.
Truth and courage aren't always comfortable, but
they're never weakness."* — Brené Brown

Human beings crave connection. There have been countless studies worldwide on what happens when we are restricted from or limited in human interaction. A simple Google search for "impact of solitary confinement" reveals that this is a hot topic with extensive medical research. The reason I bring this up is because part of our recovery is rebuilding healthy, loving relationships with others. One of the most significant ways we do this is by stepping into the light so that we can be seen for the wonderfully, beautifully flawed creatures that we are—trusting that we will not be judged for our dark side. This step is about embracing that trust and leaning into vulnerability.

I knew there were other alcoholics out there, but I never truly understood the power of being vulnerable. The power of admitting to someone else how fucking hard it was to recognize that I needed to get sober. Sharing your story with someone helps you continue your shadow work, release the stories from your past, and accept your shadow as an integral part of who you are. It reminds you that when you choose, every single fucking day, to step into the light and follow your spirit guides, ancestors, deities, or the universe, the darkness doesn't vanish. Instead, it's replaced with the conscious choice not to feed your addiction. The shadows remain, but they no longer have power over you—they become reminders of what you've overcome.

Speaking of choices, you have the power to decide with whom you share your story. I strongly believe there is power in sharing it with more than one person, so here are some considerations to help you make that decision with intention and care.

One excellent option is to share your story with a therapist. Even if they aren't specifically familiar with recovery, a good therapist will have experience with the types of challenges that surface when we get sober. Here are a few reasons why I'd recommend connecting with a therapist:

- **PTSD**: Many addicts have experienced trauma, sometimes dating back to childhood or resulting from living with another addict. Once you get sober, you may realize that your addiction was a way to cope with this trauma. Now, without that buffer, all those triggers need new coping mechanisms. Therapy provides a safe space to unpack those triggers and develop healthier responses.

- **Anxiety**: When I first got sober, my anxiety levels were off the charts. I spent countless hours obsessing over the future, trying to plan every single detail. It led to restless nights and chewed-up fingernails (and yes, I still catch myself doing this sometimes). That's why I still see a therapist—to talk through the anxiety-driven stories my mind spins. Sobriety didn't erase my anxiety, but I no longer hit those 8/9/10 levels of panic.
  - *Side note*: I originally drafted this chapter two years into recovery. Now, five years sober, my anxiety rarely spikes, and when it does, I know how to manage it. It's a blessing.
- **Depression**: If you deal with depression or have experienced suicidal thoughts, working with a therapist is essential. Recovery means facing the things that happened during your addiction head-on. These realizations can trigger intense regret, shame, and self-loathing. If you've struggled with depression before, a therapist will be crucial in helping you navigate these emotions and find pathways to healing.
- **Anger**: You may also find that anger surfaces during recovery. In my journey, I realized I harbored deep-seated anger toward my parents. It took me time to understand that I had never set healthy boundaries, which led to feelings of shame, guilt, and resentment that manifested as anger. My therapist was instrumental in teaching me how to set and maintain those boundaries, a skill that transformed my relationships and emotional well-being.

Another excellent option for sharing your story is with another recovering alcoholic. In AA, this might be your sponsor, but if that's not your thing, find someone who has a few years of recovery under their belt. Here's why this can be profoundly beneficial:

- **Tips and Tricks**: They'll have practical advice for navigating situations like your first social outing, wedding, or funeral. They've likely been there, done that, and can share what worked for them, saving you from feeling unprepared or alone in these new scenarios.

- **Sober Power**: (Yes, I totally did a little fist bump just now.) Talking to someone who's been through recovery is a powerful reminder that you're not alone. It's comforting and empowering to know there are others who recognized their lives were spiraling out of control because of addiction and chose recovery. There's a certain strength in shared experiences that lifts your spirit when you need it most.

- **New Friends**: Let's be real—not all of your old friends will be thrilled about your sobriety. And if they're not, they weren't true friends to begin with. Connecting with another recovering alcoholic will help you form new bonds with people who truly understand you. Your beautiful, evolving self deserves a circle that uplifts and supports you unconditionally.

- **Experience**: You'll be able to witness firsthand the life someone else has built in recovery and learn from their successes and mistakes. While figuring things out for yourself has its place, having tangible proof that building a life beyond addiction is possible is incredibly motivating and reassuring.

- **It's Free**: While therapy is a fantastic option if you have access to it, not everyone does. Finding someone else in recovery to talk to doesn't cost anything, making it an accessible way to build your support network.

However, there are certain people you should be cautious about relying on as your only confidants—specifically, close friends or partners. Here's why:

- **Co-dependency**: Often, when we're deep in addiction, we surround ourselves with people who feed into our habits. Close friends or partners may be part of that cycle, even without realizing it. Sharing with them exclusively can reinforce unhealthy patterns.
- **Potential for Abuse/Manipulation**: Addiction sometimes masks or helps us cope with emotional abuse in our relationships. If you share your story with someone who has been manipulative or abusive, they may use that information against you, even subconsciously.
- **Emotional Limitations**: If your close friend or partner hasn't experienced addiction themselves, your story might trigger their own insecurities or unresolved issues, leading to feelings of guilt, shame, or resentment. They may not have the emotional maturity or capacity to respond in a way that supports your recovery.
- **Their Healing**: Addiction impacts the whole family. Even if they don't realize it, they likely need to embark on their own healing journey. You do not want to tie your recovery to their progress, as doing so can lead to frustration and

disappointment. You need your path, and they need theirs.

Actionable Witchy Tasks

To wrap up this chapter, let's bring the focus back to your Magickal practice. Sharing your story is not just an emotional and mental act; it's a sacred ritual that connects you to your higher self and strengthens your recovery. Now that you've explored whom you might share your journey with, it's time to anchor those thoughts with some witchy action steps.

✳ ✳ ✳

Journal Prompts

Find a quiet space, grab your journal, and reflect on these prompts:

- *What emotions come up for you when you think about sharing your story with others? Be honest about any fears, excitement, or resistance that arise.*
- *Who in your life feels safe enough for you to share your journey with? What qualities do they possess that make them a supportive choice?*
- *What boundaries do you need to set to protect your energy while sharing? Reflect on what you're willing to share and what remains sacred.*

Writing an Intention

After journaling, craft an intention to empower your next steps:

On a piece of paper, write: *"I choose to share my story with those who will hold space for my light and shadow. I am safe, supported, and ready to step into this act of courage with my Magick intact."*

Fold the paper three times toward you to draw in the energy of support and courage. Place it under a candle (white for protection, pink for self-love, or blue for communication) and light the candle. Spend a few moments visualizing yourself confidently sharing your story, feeling seen, heard, and accepted.

Optional Ritual

For those who wish to take it further, try this small ritual:

- Gather a bowl of water, a pinch of salt, and a clear quartz crystal (for clarity).
- Mix the salt into the water, saying: *"With this salt, I cleanse my doubts and welcome clarity."*
- Hold the crystal in your hands, close your eyes, and repeat the intention you wrote.
- Dip your fingers in the water and sprinkle it around your space as a blessing, symbolizing that your story, when shared, spreads healing not just for you, but for others.

These Magickal actions will help ground your intention and support you as you step into the light of vulnerability and empowerment in your recovery journey.

CHAPTER SIX: LETTING THE LIGHT SHINE

To create a life of your highest purpose, you must first release what holds you captive. Only then can your Magick rise and manifest your truest desires.

A t this point, you are nearly halfway through all the steps. The work you've completed so far is significant, as it has allowed you to accept your past for what it truly is—something that has brought you to where you are today. It's something you've recognized no longer serves you, but most importantly, it's something from which you now have the opportunity to learn and no longer suffer. Now, it's time to begin creating the life you were meant to live!

This is where the Magick truly starts to come into play. This chapter is about harnessing your inner power and beginning to use Magick to create the life you were promised. The spells and rituals in this chapter could involve releasing what no longer serves you, creating new pathways, or manifesting your deepest desires. I'll walk you through how to uncover what you may want to create a ritual or spell for, and then I'll guide you through the process of crafting your own spells.

If, for some goddessforsaken reason, you haven't picked up a journal yet, do it now. This chapter is about transformation. It's about letting your light shine, letting go of the darkness behind you, and stepping boldly into the light you so fucking deserve.

Letting Go

Start by writing down all the things you want to let go of and leave behind. Imagine it's a new moon ritual. What beliefs or stories about yourself do you want to tear out of your life's book and throw away? These could be stories you've told yourself or stories others have written for you. I know I'm constantly rewriting my own stories. Even while writing this book, I had to confront and discard the belief that writing was difficult for me. For some reason, I held onto conflicting stories—one that I was good at writing and another that it was hard. Every time I sat down to write, I struggled. But I knew how important this book was, so I let go of that belief to push forward. **What beliefs or stories have you told yourself that aren't serving you anymore?**

Identifying Your Habits

Think about your habits. Which ones no longer serve you? Are you a perpetual procrastinator who thrives on chaos, always leaving things until the last minute and risking your reputation?

Or are you, like me, a nail-biter driven by anxiety? I'll admit, even as I write this, I still struggle with that habit. It's something I know I need to change. Letting go of habits that don't serve us is hard, but crucial. Drinking was the biggest habit I had to release. It was my go-to for celebration, self-soothing, and numbing on difficult days. But I realized that to fully embrace my spiritual journey, I needed to let go of that habit.

Take a moment to reflect on your habits and recognize those that have kept you bound. Write them down. Understand their impact and how they may be tied to your triggers or patterns.

Recognizing People to Release

This might be one of the hardest parts—realizing which people you need to let go of and leave behind. During our addictions, we often surround ourselves with people who support those behaviors: friends we partied with, acquaintances we met through substances, or even people who feed other unhealthy habits like gossiping. This can be painful, but it's essential to recognize that even if you ask these people to align with your changes, you can't expect them to. Their low vibrational energy can pull you down if you keep them around.

I was dating a lovely man named Keith when I first stepped into recovery. He had his own battles with addiction. I wish I could say we both stayed in recovery and lived happily ever after, but that's not what happened. The 2020 pandemic hit him hard, and he relapsed, abusing a prescription of Adderall. This spiraled into a severe mental breakdown, leading to multiple hospitalizations over a year. Despite our many conversations and his therapist's advice, he resisted the treatment he needed.

I eventually realized my recovery was at risk and gave him an ultimatum: he had six months to seek treatment—be it therapy, group support, AA, or NA—or he had to move out. The six months passed, and he still refused to take responsibility for his health. I reached my breaking point and asked him to leave. It was painful and messy, but I am so grateful for the friends and family who supported me. Without them, I might have caved and taken him back. Less than two weeks after we broke up, he relapsed into heroin use. I was heartbroken and grieved for weeks, but eventually, a sense of peace settled into my heart.

Manifesting What You Want

Now that you've identified what to release, it's time to focus on what you want to bring into your life. Think about your health. Have years of drinking added pounds to your waistline or affected your physical well-being? Is it difficult to lose weight or get good results at the doctor's office? Maybe your mental health has suffered, and you're battling anxiety or depression. Healing your mind and body should be a priority.

Some of us were high-functioning alcoholics or addicts who never struggled with holding down a job or paying bills. But ask yourself: **are you genuinely happy with your work?** Do you wake up excited for what you do every day? If not, now is the time to consider manifesting a new job or even a complete career change.

Reflect on Your Relationships: Consider the most intimate relationships in your life, such as your significant other or best friends. Are they supporting you in the way you need? Are they encouraging your growth and helping you be your best self?

Defining Your Life's Purpose

Once you've completed the above exercises, take the time to write down what you want your life's purpose to be. This is your new beginning, so think big. What would you be doing, thinking, feeling, or looking like in one year, five years, and ten years? No matter where you are now, envision the path you want to follow.

Creating Your Spell: Setting Your Intentions

By now, you've laid the groundwork for one of the most powerful spells you'll ever cast. I'm not going to assume you've written your own spell before, so I'll guide you through my process. And while I considered providing a spell for you, this journey is yours, and I want you to create a spell that's truly personal. Trust me when I say this will be one of the most significant spells you conduct in your entire life. Whether you realize it or not, you've already started creating it through your journaling.

Pre-Spell Work: Essential Preparations

- **Journaling Your Light**: Take the time to journal everything mentioned above. This reflection is the cornerstone of your spell.
- **Choosing a Deity**: Working with a deity is optional and personal. If you have a close relationship with one, use them in this spell. If not, meditate to see if one comes to you or invoke the universe, spirit, the creator, or your ancestors.
- **Gathering Correspondences**: Collect Magickal elements that resonate with your intentions. If you're unfamiliar

with correspondences, these are items like herbs, crystals, and colors that align with specific energies.

- o **Herbs/Incense for Cleansing**:
    - Sage, Palo Santo, Cedar, Lemongrass, Rosemary
- o **Crystals/Stones for Healing and Protection**:
    - Protection: Black Tourmaline, Obsidian, Smokey Quartz, Selenite
    - Healing: Amethyst, Amber, Rose Quartz, Green Aventurine
- o **Colors**: Use colored candles that align with your intentions:
    - White, Green, Blue
- o *Note*: Include items that represent the deity you're working with, if applicable. Don't hesitate to add your regular spell components as you see fit.

Writing the Spell

Now we get to the fun and exciting part—the spell writing itself. Writing a spell can seem intimidating at first, so here are some things to consider as you start the process:

- **Do the Pre-Work**: Don't skip the research and preparation. Dedicate 1-3 hours to gather enough information, especially if you plan to work with a deity. Consult with people in your circle if needed; they might have insights on which deities align with similar Magick.
- **Be Creative**: Remember, there is no "right" or "wrong" way to write a spell. This is your work, so infuse it with your energy and what feels natural to you. Are you an incredibly sensual being? Consider incorporating sex Magick into

your spell if that resonates. Don't hold back; the more you make this spell a reflection of you, the more powerful it will be.

- **Find Your Confidence**: This is not the time to doubt yourself. Magick comes from within, not an external source. If you're still battling stories about your power, work on rewriting them. You might need to do additional ego work or strengthen your solar plexus chakra before starting.

- **Invite Others**: Yes, this is a personal spell, but if you have supportive witches around you, invite them to join in. The more energy you put into the spell, the more powerful it will be, and the collective energy of others can amplify your intentions and help you manifest more effectively.

- **Write It Down**: Don't skip this step. Your spell should be written down, and not just on a random piece of scrap paper. Document it in your Book of Shadows or on a special piece of paper that you can reflect on in the future. This will allow you to revisit, revise, or redo the spell as needed. Remember, this spell should be uniquely yours, so let your creative expression flow in the language, correspondences, and structure.

- **Use Your Intuition**: If you find yourself stuck or unsure about what to write or what the next step should be, pause and meditate. Ask the deity or spirit guides for guidance, or simply listen to your inner voice. Pay attention to any synchronicities or messages that come up as you write your spell.

- **Thank the Universe**: Don't forget to express gratitude at the end of writing your spell. Whether you are thanking the universe, spirit, a deity, or your ancestors, acknowledgment is vital. Spellwork is a collaborative effort between you and the divine forces at play, so take a moment to appreciate that connection.

Spellcrafting

A Basic Structure of a Spell

There is no right or wrong way to write one. Your spell should be a reflection of your journey and intentions. However, to help you get started, here's the basic structure I use when crafting spells in my Book of Shadows, along with examples from a spell I created for a friend's new home.

- **The Title**: Start with a title that clearly states the intention of the spell.
  - *Example*: Cherokee New Home Spell
- **Deity**: Name the deity you're invoking, if applicable.
  - *Example*: The Great Spirit
- **Correspondences**: List the items you'll use and their intentions.
  - *Example*:
    - Herbs: Bay leaf to burn with intentions written on it.
    - Incense: Dragon's blood for strength and Patchouli for a safe and welcoming home.
    - Symbols to inscribe: Sun for happiness, Wheel for movement, Arrow to ward off negative energy.
    - Day of the week: Thursday, to support manifestation.
    - Moon phase: Full moon or waxing gibbous for power.
    - Additional items: A white candle to inscribe, a bowl of water for ashes, an athame or pin for carving symbols, and matches or a lighter for lighting.

Instructions: Outline the steps for conducting the spell. This should include all actions and any incantations you might need.

- *Example Instructions*:
    - Gather all your supplies and set up your altar.
    - Open your circle and invite The Great Spirit to join you in the spellwork.
    - Light your incense and call upon your ancestors by name to lend their power to the spell and ensure the home is safe and welcoming.
    - Carve the symbols on the white candle with your athame or pin, asking The Great Spirit to bless the home with happiness, ease of transition, and protection from negative energy.
    - Write your home desires on the bay leaf (use multiple leaves if necessary) and ask The Great Spirit to bring forth your ideal home.
    - Light the candle while reciting a candle-lighting incantation.
    - Burn each bay leaf while repeating your home desires, allowing the ashes to fall into the bowl of water.
    - Recite a closing incantation, repeating your desires and expressing gratitude to The Great Spirit and your ancestors.
    - Close your circle.
    - Store the water in a jar. When you find a home you love, pour the water in the yard and say, "This home is perfect and more than fine; with all of my intentions set, this home will be mine."

Creating Your Own Incantations

As seen in the instructions above, crafting your own incantations is an important part of spellwork. These words carry your intentions and infuse the spell with your personal energy. While I won't write incantations for you here—since they should be personal and unique—I encourage you to let your creativity flow when creating them.

Spellcrafting is deeply personal and should be tailored to your journey and desires. Trust yourself and your Magick, and know that the work you put in will be reflected in your results. Remember to revisit and adjust your spells as you grow; they can be living, evolving rituals.

Final Thoughts on Spell Creation

As you close the chapter and take a moment to reflect on the spell you've written, acknowledge the profound journey you've embarked on. You've faced your past, released what no longer serves you, and set powerful intentions for your future. This is where the true transformation begins. But writing a spell is only half the Magick; the next step is bringing it to life.

In Step 7, I'll guide you through moving from spellcrafting into spellcasting. This is where the energy you've woven into words and correspondences takes form in the physical realm. You'll learn how to channel your power, raise energy, and direct your intentions outward so that the universe can work alongside you in manifesting your desires. This is the moment when all your preparation and inner work ignite, and your Magick begins to flow.

So, take a deep breath, center yourself, and get ready to step into the next phase. It's time to move from crafting your spells to casting them with confidence and purpose. Your journey is only just beginning, and the life you're creating is closer than ever. See you in Step 7!

CHAPTER SEVEN: GETTING DOWN TO MAGICKAL

Magick begins where intention meets unwavering belief. To create the life we desire, we must first see it, feel it, and know it as if it already is.

I n traditional 12-step programs, the seventh step humbly asks a higher power to remove our shortcomings. But as witches, our power comes from within, taking the form of Magick. This step isn't about passively waiting for change—it's about actively channeling our intentions into reality. Here, we use the Magickal practices we've honed to breathe life into the intentions we wrote out in Step 6. This is a powerful declaration that we are not only recovering; we are reclaiming.

The Power of Emotion in Intention

Let's talk about the importance of emotion. I want you to look at what you wrote down as your intention—the desire you're working toward manifesting. Now, close your eyes and step into that vision. Imagine you've already achieved what you set out to create. What does your most amazing life look like? How do you feel? Does a sense of peace wash over you, or does joy bubble up inside? Notice the sensations in your body—the tingle of excitement, the warmth of fulfillment, the electric current of hope.

❋ ❋ ❋

Journal Prompt:

Write these feelings down. Be as specific as possible. If, for some reason, you find it hard to connect with these emotions, don't rush. Sit with it until you can feel it in your bones. This emotional charge is what makes intentions powerful. As witches, we know that spell work needs more than just words; it needs to be driven by raw, unfiltered emotion.

There were times when I felt completely disconnected from my intentions. It was those moments when I had to dig deep, close my eyes, and picture myself in that desired life—feeling it, tasting it, living it. I remember standing in my kitchen one morning, staring at the sunlight streaming through the window, feeling like life was both too loud and eerily quiet at the same time. I had to pause and call that vision back to mind, reliving the emotions of a life where I was fully free, unburdened, and filled with vitality. That was the moment I realized how crucial it was to keep revisiting those emotions; they were my anchor, a reminder that I am not only capable but powerful.

And when you feel off-track, this practice will ground you back to that moment—the moment you crafted your spell with every ounce of your soul. Remind yourself that as a witch, you hold within you the power to shift the course of your life. This is not a gift given lightly; it's a birthright that strengthens with every intention, every ritual, and every step taken on this path.

Reworking and Fine-Tuning Your Spell

Once you've connected deeply to those emotions, re-read your spell. Yes, you heard me. Take another look at it, and ask yourself:

- Does your spell reflect the emotions you felt during that visualization?
- Do you need to add more detail or revise the wording to match that energy?
- Is there anything in the spell that feels hollow or disconnected from your true desire?

This is where Magick truly begins. Adjust your incantation if needed. Remember, spells are living practices—they can be tweaked, reworded, and personalized as you grow and align deeper with your intention.

This step isn't just about perfection; it's about authenticity. You are a powerful witch with the capability to weave your own destiny. Each refinement to your spell is a stitch in the fabric of your reality, binding your will and energy into a force that cannot be denied.

Preparing to Cast

Now, let's talk about what comes next: preparing to cast. This step isn't just about lighting candles and saying words; it's about preparing your whole self, mentally and spiritually. This is a moment where you're not just a person in recovery—you're a witch summoning your power.

- **Inviting Others**: If you plan to cast with others, give them notice—at least a month if possible. They don't need to bring elaborate supplies, but they should come with the right mindset. I've learned that communal spells carry unique power, but only when everyone involved is attuned to the same intention. About a week before your gathering, remind them of the date, time, and purpose. And during that week, incorporate a simple daily prayer or meditation for them. Call on the universe to bless them, protect them, and guide them to show up in harmony.

- **Solo Work**: If this is a personal spell, make sure you're in the right emotional state. One morning, I felt anxious and frustrated—I knew it wasn't the right time to cast. I paused, played some music, danced barefoot in my living room, and didn't come back to the spell until I felt light and powerful again. If you're feeling low, take time to raise your vibration. Trust me: casting at a low frequency is like trying to ignite wet wood—it won't catch.

- **Ritual Bath Preparation**: While not required, a ritual bath is one of my favorite ways to cleanse my energy before casting. On the day of your spell, draw a bath infused with your favorite herbs or oils, light a candle, and let the water wash away any stagnant energy. Picture the water taking away the stress of the day, leaving you open and receptive.

Ritual Suggestion: Add elements like lavender or rosemary for cleansing, light an incense stick, and place crystals around the bath. Step into the water, feel the warmth surround you, and set your intention. Let the steam carry your prayers upward. You are preparing not just your body, but your spirit, for the Magickal work ahead.

Choosing Your Casting Location

I get it—finding the perfect spot to cast your spell can feel overwhelming, especially if you're still in the broom closet. Here's the thing: it doesn't matter where you cast, as long as you won't be interrupted. I've cast spells in my bedroom, my living room, and once in my car when I desperately needed a moment of clarity. The point is, choose a space where you can focus without disruption. Your altar could be a corner of your room or even an imaginary space you hold in your mind. The sacred space you create holds power not because of where it is, but because of the energy you bring into it.

Remember: You're not just preparing a space; you're creating an environment for your Magick to unfold. The Magick comes from you.

Choosing to Repeat vs. HAVING to Repeat

Remember how I told you to write your spell down? Here's why: spells can be repeated. You might choose to do this because you find strength in revisiting the ritual, or because life changes and so does your need for reinforcement. Personally, my daily ritual —built from recovery spells—has been my lifeline. Repeating it helps keep my past where it belongs, strengthens my resolve, and pulls me back into alignment.

Pro Tip: If your spell is complex, break it down. Pull a small incantation or verse that you can repeat daily. This bite-sized spell can be a morning mantra or something you whisper before bed.

Repeating your spell is not just about the act itself; it's about reminding yourself of your power. It's about reinforcing that you are capable of creating change in your life, that each time you repeat that incantation, you are solidifying your intention in the universe.

And let's be real: relapse can happen. I've had two within the same year, my last one on my 40th birthday. That second one was my wake-up call. It was the moment I realized that staying sober wasn't just about willpower; it was about embracing who I truly am—a witch with a purpose and a path. Relapse doesn't mean failure; it means there's more work to be done. If you find yourself slipping, show compassion for yourself. Go back to these steps and see what needs more attention. Then return to your spell, repeat it, and let it guide you forward. Each time you come back to your rituals, you're reminding yourself that your story isn't over—it's evolving.

Courage to Cast and Moving Forward

You've prepared, envisioned, and infused your spell with intention. Now, it's time. Cast your spell with all the confidence you can muster, knowing that you are exactly where you need to be in this moment. Trust that your Magick is potent, your spirit is strong, and your intention is set. You are not just casting a spell; you are declaring to the universe and to yourself that you are ready for change.

But why was this step of casting daily rituals so crucial before moving on? It's because we must first nurture ourselves, protect our energy, and heal our own wounds before we can shift our focus to others. This spell work is about building a foundation of strength and resilience. When we fortify ourselves with positive energy and a clear, empowered mind, we become capable of facing the more challenging work ahead.

As we turn the page into Chapter 8, *Make Amends with Sacred Lists*, know that this next step is about reconciliation—not just with others but with the parts of ourselves that have been wounded along the way. By caring for and empowering ourselves through ritual, we prepare to acknowledge where we've been and map a way forward toward true healing and balance. You're ready for it, witch. Embrace your power, and carry that confidence as you step into the work of making amends.

CHAPTER EIGHT: MAKE A LIST AND CHECK IT THRICE

*Making amends isn't just about repairing the past
—it's about clearing the energetic path for the
future, so our Magick can flow freely.*

I don't think there's anything in recovery that's easy. But if I had to pick the step that forces us to get brutally honest and deeply uncomfortable, it's this one. Some might argue that Step 4, with all its shadowy inventory work, is the hardest—but when you arrive at Step 8, you're tasked with making a list of people, places, and energies you've wronged. This isn't just about acknowledgment; it's the start of reparations.

In traditional recovery programs, they often say if you don't do Step 4 properly—if you don't fully take inventory—you'll keep circling back to it. My perspective? If you're unwilling to be honest in Step 8 and admit the harm you've caused, you'll struggle to fully embrace recovery. This step is vital.

So why is this so important? Why should we put ourselves through this difficult process?

It boils down to energy balance.

As witches, we know that Magick thrives on energy. It's the current through which our spells work, the force that brings our intentions to life. When energy is out of balance, our Magick suffers. It's like trying to draw water from a well that's half-empty. If we've created energetic disruptions through harm or dishonesty, the universe won't support our efforts to manifest change.

Let me be blunt: if all is not right with the universe, we will not manifest the changes we desire.

Some might call this karmic law. I prefer to think of it differently. Karmic law can feel rigid, like it denies our ability to change the course of what's coming. But I believe we can alter our trajectory. By acknowledging the wrongs we've done and taking action to make them right, we can restore balance—and that's exactly what this step is about.

Preparing for Step 8: Aligning Your Energy

This step requires deep honesty, and I know that can feel terrifying. It's normal to feel fear creeping in as you consider making this list. You might be thinking about the traditional notion of amends, the kind that involves face-to-face apologies. Don't let that fear paralyze you.

As witches, our ways of making amends are often different (we'll get into that in the next chapter). For now, focus on embracing honesty and writing your truth.

Align Your Throat Chakra

Since we're diving into truth, let's make sure your throat chakra is ready. My favorite way to align this energy center is by using it:

- Sing out loud or speak freely for 5–10 minutes. It doesn't have to be structured—sing nonsense, hum a made-up tune, or just talk about whatever comes to mind.
- Repeat a simple mantra outloud, "I am open and honest with myself." If you have a set of mala beads, using them and repeating it 108 times can be wonderful
- Write if singing or speaking isn't an option. Let your thoughts flow onto the page without worrying about sense or structure.

This is about clearing the blockages so honesty can pour through you.

Building the List

This is where the work gets real. You'll create a comprehensive list of people, places, and energies you've wronged—but this step also includes the harm you've done to yourself. Often, the deepest wounds we inflict are the ones we carry within.

1. Physical Harm

Think about how you may have caused physical harm to people, places, or things—including yourself. Be specific and detailed:

- Have you ever been in a physical altercation?
- Did you encourage someone to abuse drugs or alcohol?

- Have you damaged property, neglected your car, or left a place worse than you found it?

Now, turn the lens inward: how have you harmed your own body? For me, the most physical harm I've done was through neglect. In my 20s, I struggled with binge eating and didn't take care of my physical health. My asthma was so bad that I once climbed four flights of stairs to my apartment and almost passed out. I remember sitting there, gasping for breath, and realizing that I was the one who put myself in that position.

Write it all down. No detail is too small. Physical harm isn't just about others—it's about how you've treated the vessel that carries your soul

2. Emotional Harm

Emotional harm is trickier—it's less tangible but just as real. This mostly involves people, but it can extend to animals and even yourself. Ask yourself:

- Have you lied, withheld information, cheated, or gossiped?
- Did you neglect someone emotionally or break their trust?
- Did you fail to care for a pet or animal in your care?

And now, think about the emotional harm you've caused yourself. For me, this was allowing physical relationships with men who didn't love or respect me. I betrayed myself by settling for less than I deserved, convincing myself it was "enough." The emotional wounds I carried from those choices took years to heal.

Be honest about the impact of your actions on others' and your own emotional well-being.

3. Spiritual Harm

Finally, consider spiritual harm. This could involve people, places, or things—including your own spirit.

- Did you disrespect someone's beliefs or argue against their spirituality?
- Have you misused or disregarded spiritual tools or sacred spaces?
- Were there times you acted with ego, elevating your beliefs over others'?

Now, reflect on how you've treated your own spirituality. For me, this harm came from denying who I was. For years, I resisted calling myself a witch, even though every fiber of my being knew it to be true. I hid from my truth, and in doing so, I dimmed my own light.

Spiritual harm is subtle but significant. Reflect deeply here, especially on the ways you've betrayed your own soul.

Final Steps: Reviewing Your List

There's no such thing as a perfect list. It's not about perfection —it's about honesty and effort. This step isn't just an exercise in writing things down; it's about opening your heart to truths you may have been avoiding and preparing yourself for transformative growth.

Reviewing your list multiple times is essential because our memories and awareness don't always cooperate on the first try. The process of reviewing isn't just about catching things you missed—it's about deepening your connection to the work. Each time you revisit the list, you allow space for clarity, intuition, and even emotional release.

Here's why this matters:

- **Memory is layered**. Often, our initial attempt to recall harm focuses on the big, obvious moments. But as we sit with the list, smaller, quieter truths emerge. These might seem insignificant, but they hold energetic weight that deserves attention.
- **Perspective evolves**. With each review, you may see past actions differently. What once felt like a minor issue might reveal itself as something more impactful, especially as you grow in honesty and self-awareness.
- **Energetic release happens in waves**. Writing the list the first time can feel heavy. Each review gives you the chance to let go of guilt, shame, or fear, lightening the load as you prepare to take action in the next step.

Here's what I recommend for reviewing your list:

- Write your list and set it aside for a week. This gives your mind time to process and reflect without the pressure of perfection.
- Come back to it and review. Look at each item with fresh eyes. Ask yourself: Have I fully captured the harm? Is there anything else that needs to be added?
- Repeat this process a third time. Trust your intuition here. By this point, you'll likely feel a sense of completion or confidence that the list is as honest and thorough as it can be.

Think of this process as a ritual of discovery. You're not just making a list—you're building a map for your healing. Every name, place, or situation you add is a marker of where balance needs to be restored, guiding you toward restorative Magick in the next step.

Let me share an example from my own journey. On my first attempt at a Step 8 list, I focused on the most glaring wrongs: people I'd hurt, relationships I'd betrayed, and tangible harm I'd caused. But during my second review, I realized I had overlooked the harm I'd done to myself—especially spiritually. That's when I wrote down the years I'd spent denying my identity as a witch. It hit me hard to acknowledge how much I had betrayed myself, but it also brought a sense of liberation. I knew this was work that needed to be done to reclaim my power.

Why this process matters: Reviewing your list allows you to face deeper truths and build readiness for the next step. It ensures you've acknowledged not only what's obvious but also what's buried—those small, overlooked moments that hold big energy. When you take the time to sit with your list, you're honoring the sacred work of making amends.

In Step 9, we'll use this list as the foundation for intentional action. You'll craft spellwork to send healing energy to those impacted by your past actions, mending the threads of shared stories and restoring energetic balance. Every name and situation you've written down becomes a thread in the tapestry of your healing work, and by taking this step seriously, you're preparing for the powerful Magick to come.

Remember, this isn't about judgment or punishment. It's about creating a complete, authentic map to guide you toward balance and healing. With each review, you're one step closer to restoring the harmony that will strengthen your Magick and your recovery.

A Personal Reflection

As I write this, I'm reminded of my own journey with spiritual harm. Raised Catholic, I spent a lot of time in church growing up. As a young adult, I resisted seeing churches as sacred spaces, digging my heels in whenever I had to go.

I didn't realize at the time that these buildings are profoundly spiritual places for Christians. Now, when I visit a church, I bring a donation or light a candle to honor the space. It's a small way to make amends for my past dismissiveness.

This is what Step 8 teaches us: harm extends beyond the physical and emotional. It reaches into the spiritual, asking us to face truths we've ignored.

CHAPTER NINE: MAKE AMENDS THROUGH SPELLWORK

The threads of our actions are woven into the lives of others. Healing begins when we mend those threads with intention and love.

In a traditional 12-step program, making amends is presented as an essential step, often urging you to confront individuals directly—provided it doesn't cause harm. While the intent is noble, the execution has always felt a bit flawed to me. How can we really know if reaching out directly might hurt someone until we've already done it? That uncertainty has always rubbed me the wrong way.

As witches, we are uniquely equipped to approach amends differently. Instead of relying solely on subjective judgments or risking harm, we can harness our Magick to restore balance. Through intentional spellwork, we can send healing energy to those we've hurt—including ourselves. Yes, you read that right. If you've harmed yourself in the past—through neglect, self-sabotage, or destructive behaviors—you deserve to receive that same energy of forgiveness and restoration. This is about mending every thread in the tapestry of your life, and that includes the one that holds you together.

The Purpose of Spellwork Amends

Let's get one thing straight: making amends—whether through spellwork or direct action—is work. Hard work. The purpose is not just to soothe our own guilt but to genuinely rebalance the harm we've caused. If you believe in karma, think of this as a way to rewrite the energetic script before the universe sends it back your way.

But what about the harm we've inflicted on ourselves? The sleepless nights spent berating ourselves for past mistakes. The times we numbed our pain with substances instead of facing it. The moments we sabotaged opportunities because we felt unworthy. Those actions leave scars, too. And if we're being honest, it's often the hardest amends to make.

Think of it this way: when you're crafting spellwork for someone you've hurt, you're not just offering them a gift of healing—you're also clearing your own energetic field. The same applies to the harm done to yourself. By addressing that pain with compassion and intention, you're reclaiming your power, healing your wounds, and creating space for growth.

Pre-Work: Your "Book of Amends"

Before diving into spellwork, preparation is key. I recommend dedicating a journal specifically to your amends work—let's call it your Book of Amends. This is where you'll document your process, reflect on your actions, and map out your intentions. Here's how to start:

Step 1: Identify the Individual or Yourself

Choose one person at a time. Don't overwhelm yourself by trying to tackle everyone at once. Use your intuition or connect with your spirit guides to select the first person—or reflect inwardly and consider if you need to be the first on your list.

Step 2: Write Down the Details

For each individual—or for yourself—include:

- How you harmed them (or yourself): Be as detailed as possible. If privacy is a concern, use shorthand only you understand. For example, "Lied about XYZ" or "Ignored self-care for months" are good starting points.
- Their (or your) current life situation: Are they thriving, or are they struggling? Are you still dealing with the fallout of your own past decisions? This helps guide the type of healing energy you'll send.
- Their (or your) passions or causes: If their life is thriving, consider supporting something they love. If it's for yourself, think about what you've neglected that would bring you joy and restoration.
- Your current relationship: If your bond is strong, consider an in-person amends. If not—or if it's yourself—Magick from afar (or inwardly) works just as well.

Step 3: Plan Your Spellwork

- Describe the type of spell: What specific energy or healing are you sending? Are you casting a spell for their health, success, or emotional well-being? For yourself, what do you need most—clarity, self-forgiveness, or courage?
- Action steps: Write a clear, detailed plan for executing the spell. Include everything from gathering tools to timing. This ensures you're fully prepared to approach the work with intention.

When Not to Perform Amends Work

Let's talk about a big one: when you're not ready to perform amends work. If you're hesitating, stalling, or justifying your inaction, it's often a sign that your ego is in the driver's seat. And let me tell you, your ego has a way of making everything about you instead of the healing you're trying to offer.

Here's an example: Imagine you've written out the details of how you harmed someone and are ready to create a spell to help mend that connection. But instead of focusing on the harm caused, you start thinking things like, "They probably don't even remember this. Maybe it wasn't such a big deal. Besides, I'm a different person now." That's your ego talking. It's trying to protect you from discomfort by minimizing the impact of your actions.

Another red flag? If you catch yourself thinking, "If I do this, they'll finally see how much I've grown, and they'll have to forgive me." Nope. This is not about winning points, proving your worth, or getting validation. This is about clearing energy and creating healing, not stroking your ego.

When you notice these patterns, take a step back. Return to Step 4: Align with Truth and Shadow. Revisit your inventory and ask yourself:

- Am I being fully honest about what happened?
- Am I prioritizing their healing, or am I focused on my own comfort?
- Am I making excuses because I'm scared of facing the truth?

You're not a bad person for feeling these things—it's part of the process. But you owe it to yourself and those you're trying to make amends with to approach this work with a clear, honest, and humble heart.

Distance Spellwork Amends: When Not to Approach Directly

Sometimes, approaching someone directly to make amends is not the right choice. Maybe the relationship is too strained, or the person has explicitly said they don't want to hear from you. Here's a story to illustrate:

A witch in recovery—let's call her Dani—once shared how she wanted to apologize to an ex-partner she had hurt deeply. They had parted ways years ago, and she had since realized how her actions had contributed to the pain they both carried. But when Dani reached out, the ex made it clear they didn't want contact. It was a harsh pill to swallow, but Dani honored their boundary and shifted her focus to distance spellwork. She crafted a ritual that sent them healing and peace, without needing their involvement.

The lesson? If someone has communicated that they don't want to engage, respect that. Making amends isn't about forcing your way into someone's life—it's about repairing energy in a way that honors everyone's needs.

Distance spellwork can also be the right choice if the person is in a vulnerable place, such as dealing with illness, grief, or their own recovery journey. Your intention is to heal, not to burden them further.

Grounding Between Spells: How to Know and What to Do

Performing spellwork amends can be incredibly draining, both emotionally and energetically. But how do you know when it's time to pause and ground yourself? Here are some signs to watch for:

- You feel physically exhausted or lethargic after completing a spell.
- Your emotions feel heightened or unstable, like you're on the verge of tears or snapping at someone.
- You have trouble focusing or feel "scattered" in your thoughts.
- You notice physical sensations like headaches, nausea, or tightness in your chest.
- You start doubting the effectiveness of your work or feel like you're spiraling into guilt.

When you notice these signs, it's time to hit pause. Here are five ways to ground yourself between spells:

Get Outside

Walk barefoot in the grass, sit under a tree, or simply feel the breeze on your skin. Nature has a way of recalibrating your energy.

Engage in Physical Movement

Try yoga, stretching, or even dancing. Physical movement helps release stagnant energy and gets you back into your body.

Use a Grounding Tool

Hold a grounding stone like hematite or black tourmaline, or light an earthy incense like patchouli or sandalwood. Focus on the sensation or scent to center yourself.

Take a Salt Bath

Salt is incredibly cleansing and grounding. Add some Epsom salt to your bath, along with a few drops of essential oil like lavender or cedarwood, and soak while visualizing negativity leaving your body.

Eat Something Earthy

Foods like potatoes, root vegetables, or even a simple piece of bread can help you feel more rooted. As you eat, visualize yourself connecting with the earth.

Remember, grounding isn't just about recovery—it's about self-care. Taking the time to center yourself ensures that you can show up fully for the next step of your journey.

Moving Forward: A New Layer of Healing

Healing through intentional spellwork is a deeply transformative practice, but it's only one part of the journey. As you mend old wounds and clear energetic ties, new challenges and shadows may arise. This is where the next step, Sustain Growth with Ongoing Shadow Work, comes into play.

Shadow work isn't a "one and done" process. It's a lifelong practice of exploring your hidden corners, facing discomfort, and growing stronger because of it. In the next chapter, we'll dive into how to use shadow work as a tool for sustaining growth, finding renewed purpose, and using your experiences to uplift both yourself and others. Each step builds on the last, creating a Magickal tapestry of healing and transformation.

Recovery isn't about perfection—it's about progress. With each spell, each act of forgiveness, and each moment of self-reflection, you're creating space for a brighter, more aligned version of yourself to emerge.

CHAPTER TEN: SUSTAIN GROWTH WITH ONGOING SHADOW WORK

The shadows we fear are not here to harm us—they are here to teach us. By stepping into the darkness, we uncover the light within ourselves.

By now, you've probably figured out that recovery is some seriously intense shadow work. Actually, it's the most intense shadow work I've ever done in my life. And Step 10? It's your call to embrace shadow work as a lifelong practice. If you're wondering why this is crucial, let me break it down.

Shadow work helps you spot patterns—especially the ones that don't serve you. You know, those sneaky behaviors that drag you down, dull your Magickal power, and—let's be real—could lead you back to drinking or using. When you lean into the discomfort of a craving or listen to that pesky addiction demon whispering in your ear, you begin to understand your triggers. Sitting with that uncomfortable energy lets you pinpoint what needs healing—and sometimes, that means jotting it down and coming back to it when you're stronger.

It also helps you set boundaries—both with yourself and others. Maybe you choose to avoid certain situations because they're too triggering, or maybe you distance yourself from people who pull you toward your old habits. For me, shadow work led to a hard but necessary truth: I can't be with a partner who drinks. My past taught me that when someone close to me indulges in my old vices, I'm more likely to fall into the same trap. That realization came from sitting with the raw, uncomfortable truth and letting it guide me.

But here's the thing—leaning into those moments doesn't just suck. It transforms them. Those gut-wrenching feelings can become powerful perspectives. The universe is always trying to bless us, even if the lessons arrive wrapped in pain.

This morning, as I poured my coffee, I smiled. Those uncomfortable moments? They've become a signal that I'm evolving. They whisper, "Keep going. Greatness is right around the corner."

Shadow Work Tools for Recovery

Shadow work is the backbone of recovery. It's the practice of facing your inner demons, unpacking past wounds, and growing into your highest self. While this work isn't easy, the tools you use can help make it more manageable—and dare I say—even empowering. Below are my favorite ways to dive into shadow work, each expanded with actionable insights, vivid storytelling, and guidance to make them your own.

❅ ❅ ❅

Journal Prompts

Intuitive writing is like sitting down for a deep conversation with your soul. There's no agenda, no filter—just raw, honest exploration. It's helped me make sense of my triggers, uncover patterns, and sometimes even call myself out on my own bullshit (lovingly, of course). When I was navigating early recovery, journaling became my morning ritual—a way to set the tone for my day and process lingering feelings.

How to use journal prompts:

- **Set the stage.** Treat journaling as a sacred act. Light a candle, grab your favorite pen, and create an environment that feels safe and inspiring.
- **Write without judgment.** There's no right or wrong here. You might cry, rage, or laugh—whatever comes up, let it flow.
- **Revisit your entries.** Over time, your journal becomes a map of your growth. Look back to see how far you've come and what lessons still need your attention.

Prompts to guide your reflection:

- What am I really feeling right now?
- Who have I been around lately that made me feel smaller

than I truly am?

- When was the last time I allowed myself to laugh? What was I doing?
- Am I being honest with myself, or have I been biting my tongue more than I should?
- Have I been putting myself first? If not, why?
- Do I trust the universe, or am I resisting its guidance?
- Who can I call right now that I miss? Why haven't I reached out?
- What have I been avoiding that needs my attention?
- What does my inner child love to do, and how can I honor that today?
- Why is my recovery important to me, and what would life look like without it?

These prompts can be your anchor when the seas of recovery feel rough. Start with the one that resonates most and see where it leads you.

Chakra Work

The chakras—seven energy centers within the body—are a powerful lens for understanding how energy flows (or gets stuck) in recovery. Each chakra governs specific emotions, behaviors, and physical sensations. When one is out of alignment, it can show up as symptoms that signal deeper work is needed. For me, working with my chakras has been a game-changer, offering clarity and healing when I've felt off balance.

Recognizing misaligned chakras through symptoms:

- **Root Chakra (Fear & Stability):**

- o **Symptoms:** Feeling anxious, ungrounded, or stuck in survival mode. Physical signs include fatigue, financial insecurity, or chronic pain in the lower body.
- o **My story:** In early recovery, I constantly feared I'd relapse. Journaling about my fears while sitting on the ground in my backyard helped me ground myself and find stability.
- **Sacral Chakra (Boundaries & Creativity):**
  - o **Symptoms:** Difficulty setting boundaries, shame around choosing yourself, or lack of creative expression. Physically, it might show up as hormonal imbalances or lower back pain.
  - o **My story:** After realizing I let guilt drive many of my decisions, I visualized an orange bubble of energy around me when saying "no." This practice gave me confidence to honor my boundaries.
- **Solar Plexus Chakra (Confidence & Willpower):**
  - o **Symptoms:** Low self-esteem, procrastination, or feeling powerless. Digestive issues are often linked to this chakra.
  - o **My story:** I realized my perfectionism stemmed from this chakra being out of whack. Repeating affirmations like "I am enough as I am" helped me release those expectations.
- **Heart Chakra (Love & Compassion):**
  - o **Symptoms:** Difficulty giving or receiving love, feeling closed off, or holding onto resentment. Physically, this might show as tension in the chest or shoulders.
  - o **My story:** I began placing my hand on my heart during meditation, imagining it glowing green. This

simple act helped me open up to both self-love and connection with others.

- **Throat Chakra (Truth & Expression):**
  - o **Symptoms:** Struggling to speak up, fear of judgment, or lying to yourself. You might also experience a sore throat or jaw tension.
  - o **My story:** I found that small steps—like speaking up when my coffee order was wrong—helped me reclaim my voice and honor my truth.
- **Third Eye Chakra (Intuition & Clarity):**
  - o **Symptoms:** Feeling disconnected from your intuition, difficulty trusting your instincts, or overthinking.
  - o **My story:** Following my 'gut instinct' sharpened my intuition. By following whatever I was shown without question , I began to see more synchronicities and see the world around me shift.
- **Crown Chakra (Purpose & Spirituality):**
  - o **Symptoms:** Feeling lost, disconnected from your purpose, or questioning your beliefs.
  - o **My story:** Writing this book has been a crown chakra awakening, aligning me with my soul's mission and showing me how my recovery can serve others.

Actionable Step: Reflect on your own life. Where are you feeling stuck? Which symptoms resonate? Use these reflections as your guide to explore where deeper healing is needed.

When the Tools Aren't Enough

Let's get real: recovery isn't all rainbows and crystals. Early on, it can feel like the universe threw you into the deep end without a life preserver. You're trying to unlearn behaviors that might have been part of your daily life for years. And while breakthroughs can happen quickly, true transformation unfolds over time. Recovery is a journey—one you take day by day.

Here's how to navigate the tough moments:

- **Talk to someone in recovery.** Connection is your lifeline. Call a friend, sponsor, or mentor who gets it. Tell them, "I'm struggling, and I need to talk." Sometimes, just hearing someone say, "I've been there, and you'll get through this," is enough to shift your mindset.

- **Attend a meeting.** Even if you don't feel like it, showing up to an AA meeting or recovery circle can be grounding. Early in recovery, I resisted meetings, thinking I didn't belong —but every time I went, I left feeling lighter and more supported.

- **Burn your craving away.** Light a small candle (a birthday candle works great) and focus on the flame. Imagine your craving as a shadow within you, slowly dissolving into the light. This simple ritual reminds me that cravings are temporary—they don't define me.

- **Breathe through it.** The 4-7-8 breath technique is my go-to. Here's how to do it:
    - Press your tongue to the roof of your mouth.
    - Inhale deeply through your nose for a count of 4.
    - Hold your breath for a count of 7.
    - Exhale slowly through your nose for a count of 8.
    - Repeat for 9 times, releasing your craving with each exhale.

- **Personify and bind your craving.** Give your craving

a name and identity. Mine is "Drinking Demon." When it shows up, I perform a binding spell—visualizing it tied up and powerless. It's a symbolic act, but it helps me reclaim my power.

Remember: These moments will pass. Each time you choose recovery over relapse, you're building resilience. Trust the process, even when it feels messy.

Closing Thoughts

Shadow work is the thread that weaves through all aspects of recovery. It's messy, raw, and deeply transformative. With these tools, you're not just surviving the discomfort—you're turning it into growth, strength, and wisdom.

As you continue this journey, remember that every step you take toward healing aligns you more closely with your highest self. And in the next chapter, we'll explore how to connect with your guides, ancestors, and deities—those wise, loving forces ready to illuminate your path and help you navigate the shadows. Let their wisdom inspire your next steps, and trust that you are exactly where you need to be.

CHAPTER ELEVEN: PRAYER, MEDITATION, AND CONTINUED SPELL WORK

Within your daily practices lies the power to transform not just your life, but the world around you. Begin, reflect, and let your Magick shine.

B y now, you've likely experienced a whirlwind of emotions on your recovery journey. Maybe there's been anger, sadness, or even doubt. Those feelings are natural —recovery often stirs up everything we've tucked away. But I hope, somewhere in this process, you've also experienced moments of peace. Not the fleeting kind, but a deep, soul-level calm that reminds you why sobriety is the path worth walking.

Recovery is a journey, not a destination. It's about finding your rhythm, your connection, and your power. These steps are designed to guide you into a mindset and consciousness where sobriety isn't just a choice—it becomes a fulfilling, Magickal way of life.

Step 11 is all about creating daily practices that keep you tethered to your higher self, your guides, and your purpose. Think of it as building a bridge—a way to connect with divine wisdom, your ancestors, or however you define your higher power. Without this connection, it's easy to feel lost, untethered, or even tempted to return to old patterns. But with it? You're grounded, empowered, and able to face whatever comes your way.

This step isn't prescriptive. There's no one-size-fits-all. What matters is showing up and building consistency. Let's explore some practices you can adopt to connect with your guides and enrich your recovery journey.

Mantras: Words of Power

Mantras are more than just words—they're verbal spells. They carry intention, energy, and the power to transform. Think of mantras as planting seeds in the fertile soil of your mind. With repetition and care, those seeds grow into beliefs and actions that guide your recovery.

In the early days of my sobriety, I was plagued by self-doubt. My inner critic whispered constantly: *You'll never make it.* Every time I felt shaky, I'd stand in front of my bathroom mirror, look into my own eyes, and say, **"I am grateful for my sobriety."** Did I believe it at first? Not always. But as the days turned into weeks, the words began to feel real. That mantra became a talisman, something I could cling to when the cravings or doubts arose.

Here's how to create your own mantra practice:

- **Choose a mantra that resonates.** You might try:
  - **I am on the best path for my life when I am sober.**
  - **My sobriety keeps me healthy in mind, body, and spirit.**
  - **I am here for a purpose, and my sobriety supports that purpose.**
- **Place your mantra where you'll see it.** Write it on sticky notes and place them on your bathroom mirror, fridge, or workspace. Set it as your phone's lock screen.
- **Say it out loud.** There's power in hearing your own voice declare these truths. Let the words vibrate through you, anchoring their energy in your body.

When I struggled, repeating my mantra reminded me why I chose this path. It's a Magickal way of shaping reality—one word at a time.

Prayers: Asking and Gratitude

Prayers often carry a stigma, but within witchcraft, they're as universal as the elements. A prayer is simply a communication— a way to express your needs, desires, or gratitude to your higher power, ancestors, or the universe. It's a Magickal dialogue, one that invites guidance and clarity into your life.

During moments of overwhelm, I turn to my adapted Serenity Prayer. Let me paint a picture for you: I'm sitting at my altar, candlelight flickering, with the weight of my worries pressing down on me. I close my eyes and recite:

O Divine Universe, grant me the power of water to accept with ease and grace what I cannot change...

The power of fire to invoke the courage to change the things I can...

The power of air for the clarity to know the difference...

And the power of earth to ground me in my highest vibrational path.

Each word feels like an invocation, a plea to the elements to guide me. By the time I open my eyes, the heaviness has lifted, replaced by a sense of calm.

How you can incorporate prayer into your practice:

- **Write a short prayer of gratitude or request.**
  - For example: *"Thank you, Universe, for supporting me in my recovery. Please guide me toward my next step."*
- **Speak your prayer during rituals, while lighting a candle, or as part of your morning routine.**
- **Use prayers as resets during challenging moments.** They're reminders that you're not alone—that unseen forces are always by your side.

Guided Meditations: Magickal Portals to Clarity

Guided meditations are Magickal portals, leading you to the depths of your subconscious and your connection to divine wisdom. If you're feeling disconnected from your Magick or unsure of your next steps, meditation can be the key to clarity. These practices offer a gentle structure to help you quiet the noise of daily life and listen for the whispers of your intuition or your guides.

I'll never forget one particular meditation. I was in a creative workshop led by one of my mentors, Nikki. That day, I felt completely blocked—life's chaos weighed heavy, and my thoughts were scattered. Nikki began guiding us through a simple visualization, her voice soothing and intentional. As I followed her words, I found myself walking through a serene forest. I could hear the crunch of leaves beneath my feet, smell the fresh earth, and feel the cool breeze on my skin. Then, in a clearing, a glowing orb of light appeared before me—it was my guide. The messages I received during that meditation were profound, offering exactly what I needed to resolve a conflict I'd been wrestling with for weeks. I left that session feeling lighter, more aligned, and deeply connected to my path.

Where to Find Guided Meditations

You don't need a mentor or workshop to experience this kind of transformation. There are countless resources available online that can guide you into these Magickal spaces:

- **YouTube:** Search for guided meditations tailored to your needs—whether it's meeting your spirit guide, reducing anxiety, or manifesting abundance. Look for meditations that include binaural beats or frequencies (such as 432 Hz or 528 Hz) to enhance the experience. These tones are believed to align your energy and promote deeper relaxation and connection.

- **Spotify or other audio platforms**: Many playlists are curated specifically for spiritual seekers. Search for terms like *"guided meditation for clarity"* or *"binaural beats for healing."* These platforms are excellent for finding high-quality meditations that you can save and return to.

- **Meditation apps**: Apps like Insight Timer, Calm, or Headspace often have free guided meditations. Some even categorize them by theme, duration, or intention, making it easy to find what you need.

Your meditation practice can look like this:

- **Start small.** Just two minutes of quiet reflection can shift your energy. It's okay to begin with short sessions and build from there.
- **Set your intention.** Before choosing a meditation, think about what you want to achieve. Are you seeking guidance? Trying to release fear or stress? Wanting to align with your higher self?
- **Look for specific features.** Meditations that include binaural beats or specific frequencies can enhance your connection, creating a soothing atmosphere that promotes focus and relaxation.
- **Keep a notebook nearby.** Insights often come through in vivid images, emotions, or unexpected words. Writing them down can help you make sense of the messages and revisit them later.

A Few Tips for Success

Meditation doesn't need to be perfect. It's normal for your mind to wander or for some sessions to feel less impactful than others. What matters is the intention behind the practice—the act of showing up for yourself. Over time, as you build consistency, you'll find it easier to access the clarity and connection you're seeking.

Guided meditations are a gift to your recovery and Magickal practice. They provide a sacred space to pause, listen, and realign with your purpose. With so many resources available at your fingertips, it's easy to make them a regular part of your life. □

Gratitude Journals: Writing and Sharing Your Blessings

Gratitude is one of the most transformative energies you can invite into your recovery. Yes, we've covered gratitude already, and I'm bringing it up again because it is that potent and powerful. In my experience, gratitude isn't just another tool in the recovery toolbox—it's the foundation that supports everything else. When you embrace gratitude, it changes not just how you see the world, but how the world responds to you.

When I first started my sobriety journey, my sponsor gifted me a gratitude journal and encouraged me to write down ten things I was grateful for every day. At first, I'll admit, it felt forced. I'd scribble anything to fill the page: **"Coffee. My bed. The sun."** But something shifted over time. The more I practiced, the more gratitude became a natural part of my life. I began noticing it in unexpected places: in the quiet strength I found each morning, the unconditional support of my loved ones, and even my own resilience. It became a lens through which I viewed the world— and through that lens, everything seemed brighter, lighter, and more abundant.

Gratitude isn't just about writing things down—it's about feeling it. And recently, I've taken it a step further. I've started expressing my gratitude out loud, directly to the people in my life. Whether it's a friend, family member, or even a stranger who held the door open for me, I tell them how much I appreciate them and why.

Let me tell you—this practice is like spreading joy in the simplest way. Watching someone's face light up when you say, **"I'm so grateful for you"** is pure Magick. I've seen people's energy shift in an instant. A tense face softens. A weary posture straightens. It's like a ripple effect of positivity, and the best part is, it costs nothing.

Here's how you can incorporate gratitude into your life:

- **Gratitude Journaling:**
  - **Write down three specific things you're grateful for every morning or evening.**
  - **Be as detailed as possible.** Instead of *"I'm grateful for my family,"* try, *"I'm grateful for the phone call with my mom today—it made me feel loved and supported."*
  - **Over time, let this practice evolve.** You'll find yourself noticing moments of gratitude throughout the day, even before you sit down to write.
- **Express It Out Loud:**
  - **Tell someone you're grateful for them.** It could be as simple as saying, *"I'm so thankful for how you've supported me lately"* or *"I appreciate you for always making me laugh."*
  - **Start with close friends or family if it feels vulnerable.** As you grow more comfortable, you might even share your gratitude with coworkers, neighbors, or strangers.
- **Anchor Gratitude in Your Magickal Practice:**

- During your rituals or meditations, take a moment to thank your guides, the universe, or your higher self for their support.
- **Use gratitude as the energy behind your intentions.** For example, as you light a candle, say, *"Thank you, Universe, for the strength you've given me to stay on this path."*

Gratitude journals—and the act of gratitude itself—aren't just about listing blessings. They're about rewiring your mindset to focus on abundance and joy, both within and around you. They remind you of what's working, even when life feels hard, and they help you see how far you've come on your journey.

And the Magick doesn't stop with you. When you express gratitude out loud, you become a beacon of light for others. You create moments of connection, spreading warmth and positivity wherever you go. It's a simple act, but its impact is profound.

So grab your journal, think about the people in your life, and start weaving gratitude into your everyday existence. Trust me —this one practice alone has the power to transform your recovery and your Magick in ways you can't even imagine.

A Daily Ritual for Connection

During my first year of recovery, this ritual was my lifeline. Every single day, I turned to it for grounding, healing, and balance. It was simple, Magickal, and incredibly effective in helping me release the emotional and energetic blocks that were impacting my chakras. Each movement and affirmation brought good, healing energy into my being and kept me aligned with my purpose. Even now, while I've added other practices to my routine, I'll never forget how powerful this ritual was—and still is—when I need to reconnect with myself and the universe.

Here's how it flows, step by step, with each pose offering unique benefits for your energy and recovery:

Mountain Pose (Root Chakra)

"I open my chakras and allow energy to flow in, through, and out."

This pose is all about grounding. Stand tall with your feet firmly planted on the ground, toes spread wide, and weight evenly distributed. Imagine roots growing from your feet, connecting deep into the earth. This visualization anchors you, creating a sense of stability and security.

Benefits:

- **Balances the root chakra**, which governs feelings of safety, stability, and belonging.
- **Reminds you that you are grounded and supported by the universe.**
- **Helps calm anxiety and create a solid foundation for the day ahead.**

When I felt shaky in my sobriety, this pose reminded me that I was rooted in my recovery, no matter how chaotic the world around me seemed.

Yogi Squat (Root Chakra)

"I am safe and grounded."

In this pose, lower into a deep squat with your feet flat on the ground, hands pressed together at your heart center. Close your eyes and focus on your breath. Feel the strength in your legs and the connection to the earth beneath you.

Benefits:

- **Further activates the root chakra**, reinforcing your sense of security and belonging.
- **Releases tension in the lower back and hips**, areas where fear and stress often accumulate.
- **Grounds you in the present moment**, reminding you that you are safe in your sobriety.

This pose was my go-to when I felt overwhelmed. It brought me back to my body and reminded me that I could face whatever challenges came my way.

Pigeon Pose (Sacral Chakra)

"I release guilt and shame."

Move into pigeon pose by extending one leg behind you and folding the other in front, alternating sides. As you settle into the pose, focus on releasing emotions tied to guilt and shame—common feelings in recovery.

Benefits:

- **Opens the sacral chakra**, which governs emotions, creativity, and pleasure.
- **Helps release stored emotions in the hips**, a common area where we hold guilt and shame.
- **Encourages emotional release and acceptance of past**

mistakes.

In this pose, I often felt tears come to the surface, and I let them flow. Each time, I emerged feeling lighter, freer, and more connected to my healing.

Child's Pose (Third Eye Chakra)

"I pray and express gratitude."

Kneel on the ground, lower your torso over your thighs, and stretch your arms forward. With your forehead resting on the mat, close your eyes and take deep breaths. This is a posture of surrender and reflection.

Benefits:

- **Activates the third eye chakra**, enhancing intuition and inner wisdom.
- **Creates a sense of safety and support**, allowing you to connect deeply with your guides.
- **Encourages gratitude and clarity** by focusing your thoughts on what you're thankful for.

This was where I felt most connected to my guides. I would pray, express gratitude, and often feel their comforting presence surrounding me.

Cobra Pose (Heart Chakra)

"I open my heart and pray for others still struggling."

Lie on your stomach, place your hands beneath your shoulders, and lift your chest while keeping your pelvis grounded. Open your heart and visualize sending love and light to those in need.

Benefits:

- **Opens the heart chakra**, fostering compassion, love, and forgiveness.
- **Encourages empathy and the desire to support others** in their struggles.
- **Helps release feelings of resentment** and replace them with unconditional love.

In this pose, I often thought of people who had hurt me or those still battling their addictions. Sending them love and light felt healing for both them and me.

Upward-Facing Dog (Solar Plexus Chakra)

"I am healthy in mind, body, and spirit."

Transition from cobra by straightening your arms, lifting your thighs off the ground, and opening your chest toward the sky. Feel the strength in your core as you repeat affirmations.

Benefits:

- **Activates the solar plexus chakra**, which governs confidence, self-esteem, and personal power.
- **Reinforces your commitment to health and wholeness.**
- **Boosts energy** and instills a sense of strength and determination.

This pose reminded me of my power—that I was capable of staying sober, healing, and thriving.

Supported Fish Pose (Crown Chakra)

Mediate and invite messages and guidance from the universe.

Lie on your back with a bolster or cushion placed along the length of your spine, supporting you from the sacrum to the back of your head. This allows your chest to open wide while keeping your neck gently supported. Let your arms rest by your sides with palms facing up. Close your eyes and focus on your breath, inviting messages and guidance.

Benefits:

- **Opens the crown chakra**, connecting you to divine wisdom and higher consciousness.
- **Encourages relaxation, surrender, and receptivity** to spiritual insights.
- **Brings closure to the ritual**, leaving you feeling aligned and centered.

This was my favorite part of the ritual. I would often receive flashes of inspiration, clarity, or comforting messages from my guides, reassuring me that I was on the right path.

Why This Ritual Works

This 10-minute practice is more than just movement—it's an act of Magick. It helped me release negative energy, align my chakras, and start each day with intention and balance. For my first year of recovery, this was my daily anchor. It grounded me when I felt unsteady and infused me with the healing energy I needed to move forward.

Even now, though I've added other practices to my routine, I return to this ritual whenever I feel the need to reconnect. It's a simple yet profoundly powerful way to honor your body, mind, and spirit. Whether you're new to recovery or well along your journey, this ritual can become a cornerstone of your practice.

Simple Spells for Daily Support

Spells are practical tools that anchor your intentions in the physical world, protect your energy, and create boundaries when you need them most. But here's something important to remember: Magick doesn't need to be complicated to be effective. In fact, the simplest spells are often the most powerful because they allow your energy and intention to shine through without unnecessary distraction.

You are the most powerful tool in your witchcraft arsenal. You. Not your wand, your crystals, or your athame—though they're wonderful enhancements. At the core of every spell is you: a being made of water, fire, air, earth, and spirit—the very elements needed for potent Magick. Your breath is air. Your body is earth. Your blood is water. Your passion and drive are fire. And your essence, your soul, is spirit. Together, these elements make you a walking, breathing embodiment of Magick.

So, why complicate what is already perfect? With nothing more than your intention and focus, you can create spells that are just as effective (if not more so) than elaborate rituals. Let me share some simple spells that have been my go-to when life feels overwhelming.

Empath Protection Spell

"Your emotions are yours to keep; I am protected from your unwanted energy."

If you're an empath like me, you know how easy it is to absorb the emotions and energy of others. This spell is quick, simple, and incredibly effective. Close your eyes and picture yourself surrounded by a mirrored bubble. The mirrors face outward, reflecting others' energy back to them while keeping your energy safe inside. As you recite the spell, feel the bubble solidify around you, like an unbreakable shield.

Why it works:

- **The visualization anchors your intention** and creates an energetic barrier.
- **The spoken words affirm your boundary**, empowering you to hold it.
- **The simplicity ensures you can use it anytime, anywhere**, without needing tools or preparation.

I've used this spell countless times—before walking into crowded spaces, during challenging conversations, or whenever I felt drained by someone else's emotions. It's like wearing an energetic raincoat: the storm might rage outside, but you stay dry and safe within.

Lower Anxiety Spell

"Wash away my anxiety and fears to leave my mind content and clear."

This spell combines the Magick of water with the cleansing power of intention. Turn on the tap, let the water run over your hands, and focus on its cool, calming flow. As you recite the spell, visualize your anxiety swirling down the drain, replaced by a sense of calm and clarity.

Why it works:

- **Water is a natural cleanser**, both physically and energetically.
- **The act of washing your hands creates a tangible, sensory experience** that reinforces your intention.
- **The simplicity makes it accessible**—you can perform this spell in any sink, at any time.

During my recovery, I used this spell almost daily. It became a small ritual that brought immediate relief during moments of stress or overwhelm. Every time I dried my hands, I felt lighter, like I'd left my worries behind.

Boundary-Setting Spell

"This boundary is set. It will remain strong so that I feel safe, protected, and respected."

Boundaries are vital in recovery, and this spell helps you set them with clarity and confidence. Write your boundary on a piece of paper—something like, "I will not take on others' problems as my own." Hold the paper in your hands, close your eyes, and say the spell. Visualize the boundary as a glowing wall of light surrounding you, firm but flexible, allowing only positive energy to pass through.

Why it works:

- **Writing your boundary solidifies your intention**, making it tangible.
- **The spoken words empower you** to claim and uphold your

boundary.

- **The visualization reinforces the energy**, creating a protective aura around you.

This spell has been invaluable for me, especially in relationships where old patterns of codependency used to creep in. It's a reminder that my energy is mine to protect, and it gives me the strength to say "no" when needed.

Why Simplicity is Powerful

When you strip Magick down to its essence, you discover that the real power lies within you. Spells don't need to be elaborate ceremonies with a dozen ingredients and an hour-long ritual. In fact, the most effective spells often require nothing more than your intention and focus. Simplicity keeps the energy pure, allowing your own Magick to shine.

As witches, we're already Magickal beings. We carry all the elements within us, and that makes us inherently powerful. Water flows through our blood and emotions. Fire burns in our passions and desires. Air fills our lungs and fuels our thoughts. Earth grounds us in our bodies. And spirit connects us to the divine. These elements, combined with your will and intention, are all you need to cast potent spells.

Magick in Everyday Life

These simple spells have helped me navigate difficult moments with ease and clarity. They've reminded me that Magick isn't something I do—it's something I am. And the same is true for you. Whether you're protecting your energy, calming your mind, or setting boundaries, know that you already have everything you need to create the life you desire.

Keep your spells simple. Trust yourself. And remember: you are the Magick. □

Reflecting on Your Journey: Preparing for Step 12

As you complete this step, take a moment to pause and recognize how far you've come. If you've been diving into these steps— whether you've embraced every single practice or picked and chosen the ones that resonated most—you should be feeling the shifts and changes within your life. Your daily practices have helped you connect more deeply with your guides, your higher self, and your purpose. You've begun to truly understand your Magick in a profound, transformative way.

But here's the thing: this isn't just about ticking off steps on a list. It's about the journey you've been on and the growth you've experienced. Stop and reflect on that for a moment. Close your eyes, breathe deeply, and ask yourself:

- **What has changed since I started this process?**
- **How do I feel about myself and my recovery today compared to when I began?**
- **What new strengths, insights, or connections have I discovered?**

In that reflection, you'll begin to see something incredible: a story. Your story. It's the story of how you've embraced sobriety and aligned it with your Magick. It's the story of how you've faced challenges, found healing, and stepped into your power. And that story matters—not just for you, but for the world.

Your journey so far has been about self-discovery and transformation, but here's where the Magick gets even more profound: when you share your story, it becomes a beacon of hope for others. Recovery is deeply personal, but it's also communal. By sharing what you've learned and how you've grown, you create ripples of inspiration that can touch lives in ways you might never imagine.

CHAPTER TWELVE: UNDERSTANDING THE IMPORTANCE OF SHARING OUR JOURNEY

In helping others, we heal ourselves. By sharing our Magick, we light a path not just for those who follow, but for our own journey as well.

I never really knew how important this step was until recently. When I first started my journey toward sobriety and read about the 12th step, it seemed kind of weird. Why would they include this as part of the steps to recovery? Isn't recovery about me? Isn't it all about what I need to do to stay sober?

Now, I realize this might be the most important step of all. Sharing our story and journey with those trying to get sober isn't just about them—it's about us too. Every time we share, we revisit why we chose sobriety in the first place. Part of my own Step 12 is writing and publishing this book, starting Illuminate: The Unschool of Sober Witchcraft, building the Sober Witch Life Mobile App, and creating the Recovery Coven Membership. These aren't just my life's mission and purpose—they are my lifeline to my own recovery. Every single word I write, every app update I launch, every workshop I host—it all keeps me connected to my recovery and reminds me why I chose this path. These creations have been a form of service that not only supports others but continually keeps my spirit grounded and my sobriety alive.

Literally, every single time I talk to someone considering getting sober, I relive all the reasons I made this choice. I remember the chaos, the fucked-up times in the beginning. I remember how fucking hard it was. I relive those crazy floods of emotions, and I also remember the tools, tips, and tricks I picked up to stay sober. It keeps my recovery alive.

A Witch's Perspective on Step 12

But let's take this a little bit further and look at it from another perspective: a witch's perspective. This isn't much different from the traditional 12-step program's twelfth step, but sometimes seeing things from the point of view of a witch really helps to solidify why it matters. The twelfth step in many recovery programs is all about service and sharing your journey with others. For witches, it resonates on a deep energetic and spiritual level—something beyond just the practical. It's about using our Magick to lift others, and in doing so, lift ourselves. The energy we put out into the universe, the healing we share, all comes back to us in profound ways.

The Balance of Give and Take

First, the universe is in a constant balance of give and take. A constant balancing of the energy that fuels life. If you continue to give your time to other witches—to carry the message—the universe will bless you with a wonderful life in sobriety for being so giving and healing. I remember a time early in my journey when I was feeling particularly lost, and it seemed like the darkness was creeping back in. Instead of retreating, I decided to host a small circle for some witches who were struggling too. The energy that flowed during that circle shifted something inside of me. I realized that giving my time and energy wasn't draining me—it was replenishing me. Every time I give, I receive so much more in return. The universe has this incredible way of keeping everything in harmony.

Tradition of Helping Others

Second, witches have a long-standing tradition of helping others on the same path grow and learn. You can't go far in witch communities without being pulled into conversations about shadow work. And this? This is some real fucking intense shadow work. Choosing to get sober and step onto the path of recovery is probably one of the most impactful pieces of shadow work we can do. Every time the universe brings another witch into our path who could use our help, there's a good chance we'll learn something new through their journey too. I remember when I first started Illuminate, one of the first witches who joined was struggling deeply with the concept of forgiveness —both for herself and others. Walking with her through her journey helped me see aspects of my own shadow that I hadn't fully addressed. Her struggle became a mirror, reflecting back parts of myself that needed more healing. This is the beauty of our tradition—our paths are intertwined, and our growth is collective.

Strengthening Our Own Sobriety

Third, our own sobriety stays strongest when we keep it important. When we keep working on it. Guiding someone else through their shadow work is also working on our own sobriety. As we help them, we often end up reflecting on our own work or discovering another area within ourselves that needs attention. I can't count the number of times I have been in a Recovery Coven circle, offering guidance to someone else, only to feel that nudge from the universe saying, "Hey, you need to look at this too." It's in those moments of helping others that I find the most clarity for myself. It's almost like every conversation we have, every piece of advice we give, is a reminder of what we need to keep doing for ourselves. The journey never really ends, and that's what makes it so powerful.

Serving Humanity and Raising Vibrations

And finally, the universe loves to see us in service to others. Serving humanity—serving our coven—raises our vibrations and the vibrations around us. The more we do this, the higher those vibrations rise, making the world and the universe a better place overall. I've always found that after holding a group spellwork session or leading a gratitude ritual, there's this undeniable shift in energy. It's as if the universe itself is smiling back at us, acknowledging the work we're doing. One of my favorite parts of the Recovery Coven is our monthly Gratitude Ritual Circle. Watching members express their gratitude, watching the energy rise as we all contribute—it's like we're collectively adding light to the universe, one spark at a time. It's not just about us; it's about making the entire world a better place, and that kind of Magick is unstoppable.

Practical Ways to Support Other Witches

Now, you might be wondering, how can you help other witches who are trying to get sober? Let me share a few ways—earthy, practical ways:

- **Gift them this book.** If you've finished it and feel confident in your grasp of the steps, pass it on. You could buy them a new copy, sure, but your energy has already blessed this book. Seeing that it has been read could encourage them to keep going.

- **Take them to an AA meeting.** There are secular AA meetings, but they aren't everywhere. It might be more comfortable for them if a fellow witch comes along, even if you've never been. I recommend a meeting with an open talk—you can listen to someone's story together.

- **Tell them to call or text you when they're struggling.** This is one thing I've always loved about AA —the encouragement to reach out. Sometimes, a 5- or 10-minute conversation with someone who understands can get you through a craving.

- **Invite them to a sober outing.** One of the big fears at the beginning of recovery is that life will be boring. Invite them to a social activity that doesn't involve drinking and show them that we can still have fun. A few examples include attending a local witchy market, going for a nature walk, or having a movie night with witch-themed films that inspire and uplift.

- **Cast a circle with them.** If they're into ritual or communal Magick, offer to hold a circle just for them. Bring forth energies to bless them with courage and patience on their journey—courage to make the right choices, even when it's tough, and patience to take life one day at a time.

- **Create a personalized spell kit.** Gather some herbs, crystals, and a small candle, and make a spell kit specifically for their journey in sobriety. Include instructions for a simple spell focused on strength and perseverance. This not only gives them a Magickal tool to use but also shows that you've put thought and care into their journey.

- **Start a witchy book club.** Invite them and other sober witches to read books about Magick, recovery, or personal growth. Sharing thoughts and insights from these books can create a deeper bond and offer ongoing support. Plus, it provides a consistent, positive social activity that everyone can look forward to.

- **Offer to do divination together.** Pull tarot cards or runes together to gain insight into their path and any obstacles they might be facing. This can provide them with a sense of direction and reassurance, and it's also a great way to strengthen your bond and mutual trust.

- **Introduce them to the Recovery Coven.** Invite them to join our community, where they can connect with other witches who are walking the same path. Being part of a supportive group can make all the difference, especially when they see they're not alone in their struggles or triumphs. (Btw, *check the end of the book for your invitation my dear witch!*)

Conclusion: Keeping the Flame Alive

At the end of the day, it doesn't matter exactly what you do, as long as you're out there sharing your journey and helping other witches find their way. It helps them, and it helps you.

Take a moment to acknowledge everything you've done to get to this point. You've walked a challenging path, faced your shadows, and made incredible progress in your recovery journey. You should be so proud of yourself for the work you've done and the courage you've shown. Every step you've taken has led you here, and you've earned every bit of healing and growth you've achieved.

As we close this chapter, remember that celebrating our progress and supporting others is just the beginning. You've built a strong foundation, and now it's time to take that energy even further. In the next chapter, we'll dive into rituals that release and heal the collective—using our Magick to transform the universe and become beacons of hope. Let's keep the flame of recovery alive, not just for ourselves, but for everyone who needs it. Step 13 is all about engaging in rituals for universal release, sending our energy out to heal the collective and embracing our role as a beacon of transformation. Let's take this journey together and continue to shine our light.

CHAPTER THIRTEEN: THE MAGICK IN THE NUMBER 13

In the darkest of struggles, we find our most powerful light. Together, we can transform the shadows of addiction into a beacon of hope and healing.

I thought a lot about adding this chapter. For witches, the number 13 is incredibly powerful—it has Magickal properties all its own. But in the traditional world of recovery, there's a bit of a joke about Step 13. Let's get that out of the way: this isn't your joke of a Step 13. This isn't making fun of those who fall in love with the energy change that can happen when you get sober.

Step 13 in Traditional Recovery

In case you aren't aware, in traditional recovery programs, Step 13 refers to long-time members preying on newcomers. Sometimes, they take them under their wing as a sponsor and try to guide them. Other times, they start "love bombing" so the newcomer relies on them for emotional support. In other words, they're keeping the newcomer around for themselves, not for the newcomer's best interest.

And fuck, did it piss me off that they used the number 13 for that!

Why is this so dangerous? When folks first step into recovery, they are scared and vulnerable. They may also have a lot of trauma and scars they have never faced. This makes them easy targets. They're looking for a lifeline, and when someone comes along offering attention, care, or mentorship, they might not have the ability to see the red flags. They're desperate for connection, for something to hold onto. The person who preys on them might seem like a savior, but they are often manipulating that vulnerability for their own gain, which can cause deep, lasting harm to someone just starting their recovery journey.

Let me share a story about a time this happened. Someone once reached out to me for help with their nephew. Their nephew had relapsed quite a few times, even though he had two beautiful children he wanted to get clean for. When I looked into his energy, I could see an attachment on him. It sat on his shoulders and clouded his head.

A few weeks later, I was able to speak to the nephew directly, and he gave me permission to explore it further. Come to find out, he had recently gotten a new sponsor. This sponsor was throwing up all sorts of red flags, but because they were so well-known and respected in the program, the newcomer—this young man—couldn't quite see how his sponsor was impacting his energy and essentially draining him. It was clear that the sponsor's influence was not supportive; it was toxic. The nephew eventually 'broke up' with the sponsor, and he described feeling an immediate weight lift off his shoulders. Last I'd heard, his recovery was heading down the path he wanted. It's heartbreaking, but it's a reminder of why we need to protect those stepping into recovery and why Step 13, as it's often known, is so dangerous.

The Witches' Step 13

I am taking back Step 13—redefining it for what it should truly be. A powerful reminder that we witches have potent Magick that we can invoke to help combat addiction in this world. This Step 13 is the witches' Step 13. As witches, we know we have the ability to heal, and we will do regular spellwork to help release the universe from addiction.

Step 13 is about reclaiming our power, about using our Magick to heal, not harm. We are taking this number and transforming it into something that uplifts and empowers, something that brings hope and healing to those struggling. Addiction is a dark force, and we are uniquely equipped to combat it—not just for ourselves, but for the collective. We can use our rituals, our intentions, and our spells to send healing energy out into the universe, to help those who are lost in the throes of addiction, and to create ripples of transformation and hope.

Our Magick is potent, and when we come together to harness it for the greater good, we become unstoppable. This is what Step 13 is truly about: tapping into our deep well of power, our connection with the universe, and using it to make real, lasting change. We're not just talking about individual healing—we're talking about shifting the energy of the world, one spell, one intention, one prayer at a time.

The Power of Oneness

The reason this is so incredibly powerful, the reason this matters to witches, is that so many of us believe we are all connected—we are one with the universe, and the universe is one with us. Our energy is interconnected. Our physical bodies may represent us as individuals, but we are all part of a conscious collective.

So when one of us is out there suffering from addiction, all of us, in some way, shape, or form, feel it. Addiction doesn't just affect the person using—it ripples out to everyone connected to them, including those of us who are already in recovery. It could be a momentary pain in our hearts for someone we know is suffering, or we could be blindsided by a relapse. The truth is, addiction leaves scars on all of us, and even if we've found our own path to sobriety, we still feel those waves of pain, fear, and loss. We know what it's like to be in that dark place, and we feel it deeply when others are trapped there. This is why our collective Magick is so important—because when we work together to heal, we are also helping ourselves stay strong, stay connected, and stay grounded in our recovery.

Collective Healing Through Step 13

That's why, when we all commit to this Step 13—when we all embrace the power of being one and put in the work to release the universe from addiction—we're encouraging the entire human race to rise above the destruction addiction can bring. Imagine a world free from addiction: a world where people no longer need to numb their pain with alcohol, drugs, or chaos; where the destructive cycles of addiction to violence, war, gambling, and toxic relationships are replaced with cycles of healing, growth, and love.

Imagine communities thriving, individuals reclaiming their power, parents being fully present for their children, and people reconnecting with their passions and purposes. We provide more hope for ourselves and our fellow witches to rise above what holds us back and move towards our individual life purposes. Together, we can create a ripple effect of healing, and with each spell, each intention, and each ritual, we push forward to manifest a world of peace, joy, and collective upliftment—a world where our Magick becomes the catalyst for transformation, leaving behind the darkness of addiction.

Daily Rituals for Universal Release

And this can be simple. It doesn't need to be complicated. For me, it's part of my morning ritual. Every morning, I open my heart chakra and I pray for all those suffering from addiction. Whether that addiction is to drugs, alcohol, sex, violence, shopping, food, sugar, drama, or chaos—whatever is robbing these individuals of living their best possible fucking life—I pray they find the courage they need to take steps toward a life filled with more peace, love, happiness, hope, joy, and prosperity.

I pray that they find that courage every single day to keep taking those steps toward a better life. I sit, and I reflect for a few moments on any individuals I may personally know. I share their names with the universe. If I had to guess, there are probably 25 different names I recite every morning.

Other Ritual Ideas

You could also do a ritual spell once a week or once a month. If you do it once a month, I strongly encourage you to do it during a new moon. We're trying to bring forward the courage these individuals need to take those steps. Remember, these spells won't miraculously take away someone's addiction—but they can help them find courage. They can help them heal from what triggers them.

Here are five different rituals you could perform once a month:

- **New Moon Courage Invocation**: On the night of the new moon, light a white candle and set an intention for courage. Call upon the energy of the new moon for new beginnings and visualize those struggling with addiction finding the strength they need to take their next step toward recovery. Let the candle burn out completely.
- **Full Moon Release Ritual**: During the full moon, write down the names of those struggling with addiction and the specific burdens you want to help them release. Burn the paper under the moonlight, asking the universe to cleanse and transform these struggles into strength. Feel the energy of the full moon amplifying your intention.
- **Thursday Jupiter Prosperity Spell**: Thursdays are ruled by Jupiter, the planet of growth and expansion. Perform a ritual on a Thursday evening where you anoint a green candle with an essential oil like frankincense or cinnamon. Visualize those struggling with addiction expanding into

a life full of abundance and joy, free from the chains of addiction.

- **Saturday Banishing Addiction Ritual**: Saturdays are ruled by Saturn, the planet associated with banishing and discipline. On a Saturday, create a salt circle, and within it, place a black candle. Visualize addiction as a dark cloud, and as the candle burns, see that cloud dissipate and vanish. Envision those suffering finding the discipline they need to overcome their struggles.

- **Sunday Sunlight Healing Meditation**: Sundays are ruled by the sun, a symbol of light, hope, and healing. Sit outside in the sunlight or visualize the sun's rays filling you with warmth. Imagine these rays extending to those struggling with addiction, filling them with hope and clarity. Meditate on this light driving out the darkness of addiction and bringing peace.

Difference Between Step 12 and Step 13

Now, you might be asking yourself how this Step 13 is different from Step 12. I want to make sure I give you a clear answer. Step 12 encourages us to go out and talk to others who may be struggling with their addiction—to share our message, to share how we've found our sobriety and ventured into our own recovery. This book is one of those examples.

But my experience has shown me that some people aren't ready to hear those messages. Some people don't want to acknowledge they have an addiction. Some people don't see or notice that their life is filled with chaos, and that they are the common denominator. These are the people we are doing spellwork for in

Step 13.

I can't tell you how many times I see requests in Facebook groups and Reddit communities from people who have loved ones suffering from addiction. So many people tell them, "There is nothing you can do...they have to do it on their own." But come on, witches, we are powerful healers in our own right, and there are absolutely things we can do. No, we can't change them, but we can send them the energetic shifts they need to make changes for themselves.

Awakening Hope: A Community Ritual

And frankly, you may decide you want to go bigger than that. For instance, this year (it's taken me roughly four years to write and edit this book), I introduced a ritual into my community called Awakening Hope. We align it with each of the pagan holidays of the year. I take the meaning of each holiday and create a ritual that focuses not only on ridding an individual of addiction but also on healing generational lines, inner children, and the community at large.

Each of these rituals is absolutely free to attend, with one catch —it's a potluck! I was blessed with a generous donation of an Airbnb to host these, and I adore that we get to infuse that property with this loving, healing Magick that even it needs!

The very first ritual I held overwhelmed me with so much joy and gratitude that I spent the next day in tears. The energy was so powerful, so full of love and intention, that it touched me to my core. And the best part? My partner, my niece, and those who love and support me now have a way to show up and help fight the addiction that impacts so many people we care about, including me. This collective effort is what makes these rituals so profound—it's not just my Magick, but our combined energies that create true healing and transformation.

A Personal Note to You

So, my dear friend, I know the journey you've decided to take. I want you to know that you are one of those beautiful souls I pray for in my morning ritual. And if you ever need a little extra support on your journey, I'll be right here.

If You Do
Nothing Else...

CHAPTER FOURTEEN: PROTECTION AND REFLECTION: ENERGETIC FOUNDATIONS FOR THE SOBER WITCH

To protect your energy is to honor your soul. To raise your vibration is to invite the universe to dance with you.

Recovery is not a straight road. It twists and turns, with moments that feel like progress and others that feel like you're standing still. Sometimes, the steps ahead feel too overwhelming, like the weight of the world is pressing down on your chest. And you know what? That's okay.

It's okay to pause. It's okay to catch your breath. It's okay to admit that you might not be energetically ready to dive deeper into this work just yet. This isn't a failure—it's wisdom. It's your inner Magick telling you to slow down and strengthen your foundation before you build higher.

When I hit a wall in my own recovery journey, I found myself revisiting the basics: Protection and Vibration. These two practices became my lifeline when I felt unsteady, offering me the grounding and resilience I needed to move forward. If you're feeling stuck, I invite you to explore these practices. They're not just for moments like this—they're lifelong tools that will keep you rooted and rising.

Let's dig in.

Why Protection Matters

As witches, we are sponges for energy. We absorb it, feel it, and carry it—whether we realize it or not. Have you ever walked into a room and instantly felt uneasy, even though no one said a word? Or spent time with someone who left you feeling drained, like they siphoned your last ounce of energy? That's the power of external energy at work, and it can take a toll.

In my early days of recovery, I didn't realize how much the energy around me was affecting my mood. I would wake up exhausted, snap at my loved ones for no reason, and feel this unshakable sense of anxiety. It wasn't until I started working with protection Magick that I understood what was happening. My energy field was like an open door, letting in everything—good, bad, and ugly.

If you've been feeling:

- **Constant fatigue** that no amount of sleep seems to fix,
- **Unexplained anxiety** that follows you like a shadow,
- **Sudden angry outbursts** that leave you wondering, "Where did that come from?"
- **A desire to isolate**, even from people or practices you love,

You're not alone. These are signs of energetic overwhelm, and if left unchecked, they can spiral into patterns that threaten your recovery. For some, it might lead to relapse. For others, it keeps them stuck in the cycle of emotional pain.

The good news? You can stop this cycle. Protection is your Magickal shield, and it can help you take back your energy and your power.

The 3-Part Approach to Protection

Protection doesn't have to be complicated to be effective. In fact, the simplest practices are often the most powerful. When I started focusing on protection, I leaned into three core practices: **Visualizing It, Saying It, and Wearing It**.

1. Visualizing It

Your mind is an incredible tool for creating Magick. Visualization is like weaving an energetic tapestry, building a shield between you and the chaos of the world.

One of my favorite visualizations came to me during a particularly rough patch. I was feeling overwhelmed by work, relationships, and just life in general. I remember sitting on my living room floor, closing my eyes, and picturing a bubble of shimmering white light surrounding me. This bubble wasn't just light—it was warm, unbreakable, and safe. I imagined it filtering out anything harmful while letting in love and support.

Here's how you can do it:

- **Find a quiet space** and close your eyes.
- **Take three deep breaths**, feeling the air fill your lungs and anchor you in the present moment.
- **Picture a light**—bright, beautiful, and protective—starting at your heart.
- **Watch this light expand**, forming a bubble around your body.
- **Say to yourself**:
  "I am safe. I am protected. Only love may enter my energy field."

Do this each morning before you start your day, and you'll notice a shift. It's like wearing an invisible suit of armor.

2. Saying It

Words have power—especially when spoken with intention. When you say your protection aloud, you're casting a verbal spell that reinforces your energetic boundaries.

There was a time when I felt drained just walking into a room full of people. I started carrying a small script in my head, one I could say quietly or even silently before stepping into challenging spaces. It was simple:

"I call on my Magick to protect me. No harm, no negativity, no unwanted energy may enter my space. I am shielded and strong."

Try creating your own mantra or use mine. Speak it each

morning, when you feel off balance, or before entering a potentially draining environment. You'll feel the strength of your words reinforcing your energetic armor.

3. Wearing It

Sometimes, we need physical reminders of our Magick. Wearing a protective item—whether it's a crystal, a piece of jewelry, or a charm—can help you carry your intention throughout the day.

One of my favorite talismans is a necklace with a piece of black tourmaline. I enchanted it during a full moon ritual, asking it to absorb negativity and shield me from harm. Whenever I wear it, I feel an instant sense of safety, like I'm carrying a little piece of home with me.

Here are some ideas to get you started:

- **Crystals**: Black tourmaline, obsidian, or hematite are excellent for grounding and protection.
- **Jewelry**: Enchant a ring, bracelet, or pendant with protective energy.
- **Charms**: Create a pouch filled with protective herbs like rosemary, sage, or bay leaves and carry it in your pocket.

Hold your item in your hands, focus your intention, and say:

"I charge you with protection. May you shield me from harm and keep me grounded in light."

Raising Vibration

Once protection is in place, the next step is to raise your vibration. Why? Because protection creates the container, but a higher vibration fills it with light, joy, and healing. Without actively raising your energy, the container can still feel heavy, like you're shielding yourself but not thriving. High-vibrational energy attracts positivity, clarity, and resilience—everything you need to stay grounded in your recovery.

The Power of Gratitude

Gratitude is my favorite way to raise vibration because it's simple, accessible, and endlessly transformative. I've had days when everything seemed to go wrong. Days when I questioned whether I could keep going in my recovery. On one of those particularly dark days, I sat down, opened my journal, and forced myself to write one thing I was grateful for.

At first, I struggled. My mind wanted to focus on all the pain and frustration. But then I wrote:

"I'm grateful for the sunlight streaming through my window."

That one sentence broke the spell. My focus shifted. I noticed the warmth on my skin, the golden hue of the light. I wrote more:

"I'm grateful for my favorite tea."

"I'm grateful for the cat curled up at my feet."

By the time I finished, I felt lighter. The heaviness in my chest had eased, replaced by a quiet sense of peace. That's the power of gratitude—it helps you see the Magick in the mundane.

Here's how you can integrate gratitude into your daily life:

Start a Gratitude Journal

We've already discussed this, but it is so powerful we're revisiting it again. Every night, write down three things you're grateful for. They can be big or small, profound or simple. Some days you might write about loved ones or recovery wins. Other days, it might be a soft blanket or a moment of silence.

Speak Your Gratitude

Throughout the day, say your gratitude out loud. For example:

"I'm so thankful for this hot shower."

"I'm grateful for this delicious meal."

"I'm grateful for the chance to rest."

Speaking gratitude reinforces it and helps shift your focus in real time.

Make It a Ritual

During your daily or weekly Magickal practices, incorporate gratitude. Light a candle, hold a crystal, and say:

"Thank you, universe, for the blessings in my life. Thank you for the lessons I'm learning and the growth I'm experiencing."

Other Ways to Raise Vibration

Gratitude is just one tool in the vibration-raising toolbox. If you're feeling stuck, try these other practices:

- **Movement:** Dance, stretch, or go for a walk. Moving your body shifts stagnant energy and elevates your mood. I often dance in my kitchen when I feel low—it's silly, but it works!
- **Music:** Create a playlist of songs that lift your spirit. Singing along or simply listening can raise your energy in

minutes.

- **Nature**: Spend time outside, even if it's just sitting under a tree or walking barefoot on the grass. Nature has a grounding, healing energy that's hard to replicate elsewhere.

The 30-Day Energetic Reset

Combining protection and gratitude into a daily practice can create profound shifts in your energy and perspective. This reset is designed to help you feel more aligned, stable, and ready to continue your recovery journey.

Daily Practices for 30 Days

Here's what the reset looks like:

Protection Practice

- **Morning**: Visualize your protective bubble, speak your mantra, and wear your talisman.
- **Throughout the day**: Repeat your mantra whenever you feel your boundaries being tested.
- **Evening**: Reflect on any energetic challenges you faced and how your protection helped.

Gratitude Practice

- **Morning**: Say one thing you're grateful for as you start your day.
- **Throughout the day**: Notice moments of gratitude and speak them aloud.
- **Evening**: Write down three things you're grateful for in your journal.

Reflection

- **Weekly**: Set aside 10 minutes to reflect on how these practices are impacting your mood, energy, and recovery. Write your insights in your journal or share them with a trusted friend or mentor.

My 30-Day Reset Experience

When I first committed to this reset, I was skeptical. Could something so simple really make a difference? But by the end of the first week, I noticed small but significant changes. I felt less reactive, more centered, and more hopeful. By the end of the month, I was ready to dive back into the Witch's 13 Steps with a renewed sense of strength and purpose.

Reflection and Readiness

Recovery isn't a sprint—it's a journey. Sometimes, you'll feel ready to take big leaps forward. Other times, you'll need to pause and reground yourself. After completing the 30-day reset, take some time to reflect:

- **Do you feel more in control of your energy?**
- **Have you noticed shifts in your mood, resilience, or sense of connection?**
- **Are you ready to revisit the Witch's 13 Steps, or do you need more time with these practices?**

If you're not ready to move forward, that's okay. Remember, there's no timeline for healing. Every moment you spend protecting your energy and raising your vibration is a step in the right direction.

Ritual: Grounding and Protection

To integrate protection and gratitude into your Magickal practice, try this simple ritual:

- **Preparation**: Gather a white candle, your protective talisman, and a journal.
- **Visualize**: Light the candle and visualize your protective bubble forming around you.
- **Speak**: Hold your talisman and say:
  "I call on the power of light and love to protect me. I am grounded, shielded, and safe."
- **Gratitude**: Write down three things you're grateful for in your journal. Speak them aloud, feeling the vibration of gratitude filling your space.
- **Close**: Snuff out the candle, place your talisman in a safe spot, and say:
  "I am protected. I am grateful. I am whole."

Conclusion

Magick is a practice, but it's also a way of being. By focusing on protection and vibration, you're not just creating shields and lists—you're creating a life of resilience, joy, and alignment.

Remember, your journey is unique to you. There's no wrong way to recover, no wrong pace to heal. Whenever you feel lost or stuck, return to these foundational practices. They are your roots, keeping you steady as you grow.

You are protected. You are powerful. You are Magick.

CHAPTER FIFTEEN: RESOURCES FOR THE RECOVERING WITCH

Recovery is not about becoming someone new. It is about remembering who you were before the world told you who to be —and reclaiming your power, one Magickal step at a time.

R ecovery is a deeply personal journey, and for witches, it comes with unique challenges. Traditional recovery programs can offer structure and support, but they often lack the spiritual depth and Magickal alignment that many witches need to feel truly empowered. I know this firsthand because I walked this path myself. I longed for resources that honored both my sobriety and my Magick, and I struggled to find spaces where I could embrace both aspects of my identity without compromise. That longing inspired the creation of these resources—tools designed to help other witches in recovery build a foundation that feels both spiritually nourishing and emotionally supportive.

Navigating recovery as a witch means balancing the need for structured healing with the desire for deep spiritual connection. It means recognizing that sobriety is not just about abstaining from substances, but about reclaiming personal power and stepping fully into your Magick. These resources were created to give witches in recovery tangible ways to integrate their practices into their healing journey. Whether you need guidance, community, or rituals that honor your path, these tools are here to support you.

A majority of these resources are available for free, ensuring that anyone who needs support has access to it. Some require a financial exchange, which helps sustain the continued creation and maintenance of these offerings, allowing for deeper, more transformative work. But at their core, these resources exist to ensure that recovery is not about losing a part of yourself but instead about reclaiming your personal power and spiritual connection in a way that feels completely authentic.

The Role of AA and Other Traditional Recovery Programs in a Witch's Journey

For many, traditional recovery programs such as Alcoholics Anonymous (AA), SMART Recovery, Refuge Recovery, and Celebrate Recovery serve as crucial pillars of support. They provide structured guidance, accountability, and community, which can be especially helpful during the early stages of sobriety or in moments of struggle. The power of these programs lies in their consistency—they offer frequent meetings, clear steps for healing, and a framework that helps people feel less alone.

For witches, however, these programs may not always feel fully aligned with their spiritual beliefs. Many contain religious undertones or focus on surrendering to an external higher power rather than harnessing one's inner strength. That doesn't mean they aren't valuable; rather, it means that witches in recovery may benefit from a blended approach, one that allows them to take what works from traditional recovery spaces while also engaging with Magickal tools and witch-friendly support systems.

It's important to acknowledge that different paths work for different people. Some witches thrive in AA or SMART Recovery, drawing strength from the structure and community. Others may struggle to connect with the language or approach of these programs and instead find solace in personal rituals, shadow work, and energy healing. The key is to create a system of support that speaks to your soul, offering both the stability of a strong foundation and the freedom to integrate your own spiritual practices.

Magickal Resources for the Recovering Witch

Sober Witch Life Mobile App

Recovery as a witch can sometimes feel like navigating two worlds at once. On one side, there's the structured recovery path, with steps and accountability. On the other, there's the deeply personal, intuitive journey of Magick—your rituals, your energy work, your spiritual evolution. What if you didn't have to choose between the two?

The Sober Witch Life Mobile App was created as a bridge between these two worlds, offering a space where sobriety and spirituality coexist in harmony. Whether you're just starting out or have been on this path for years, this app provides the tools, guidance, and community you need to stay connected—to yourself, your recovery, and your Magick.

What's Inside the Sober Witch Life Mobile App?

The Sober Witch's Tool Kit

A collection of Magickal and practical resources designed to support your mind, body, and spirit throughout recovery.

- **The Witch's 13 Steps to Recovery** – Traditional recovery steps, reimagined through a Magickal lens, honoring intuition, empowerment, and ritual.
- **The Witch's Promises** – A framework of commitments to yourself and your journey, offering guidance for **spiritual and emotional healing**.
- **The Frequency of Acceptance** – A powerful **energetic practice** that helps you transmute low-vibrational emotions (like guilt or shame) into higher frequencies, so you can move forward with resilience.
- **The Witch's Serenity Prayer** – A grounding invocation for moments when life feels overwhelming, helping you **recenter and find clarity**.
- **Recovery Tarot and Life's Purpose Spreads** – Tools for **divination and self-reflection**, offering insights into your path and how to navigate challenges.

- **A Healing & Clearing Frequency Playlist** – Curated sounds and vibrations designed to **realign your energy**, cleanse negativity, and bring emotional balance.

The Grimoire of Recovery

A growing library of articles, spells, and rituals tailored for witches in recovery. Whether you're looking for a full moon release ritual, a protection spell against triggers, or journal prompts for shadow work, this grimoire provides practical Magick that supports both sobriety and spiritual evolution.

The Magickal Self-Care Vault

Healing isn't just about what you remove from your life; it's about what you intentionally add to support your growth. The Magickal Self-Care Vault contains live and recorded meditations, ritual practices, and educational workshops that offer guidance when you need it most. Whether you're seeking a cleansing ritual to shed old energy or a self-love meditation to reinforce your worth, this vault provides tools to nourish your soul and keep you grounded.

Sober Witches in Recovery Chat

Recovery isn't meant to be done alone. Having a community that truly understands can make the difference between feeling isolated and feeling supported and seen. The Sober Witches in Recovery Chat is a safe, welcoming space where you can connect in real-time with other witches in recovery—whether you need encouragement, want to share a success, or simply need someone to listen.

How This App Can Transform Your Recovery

It's one thing to stay sober. It's another to thrive in recovery, feeling empowered, Magickal, and deeply aligned with your spiritual path. This app provides the resources, structure, and connection to help you not just maintain your sobriety but embrace it as a source of power.

Picture yourself starting your morning with a tarot spread, gaining clarity on your day ahead. Imagine feeling grounded and supported after engaging in a full moon ritual, knowing that your intentions are being amplified by others walking the same path. Think about the confidence that comes from knowing you are not alone, that there is a community of sober witches who truly see and support you.

That's what the Sober Witch Life Mobile App is: a space to grow, to heal, to connect, and to reclaim your power—one Magickal step at a time.

The Weekly Witch's Recovery Circle

Imagine sitting in a sacred circle, surrounded by witches who truly understand the ups and downs of recovery. A space where no one judges your past, no one questions your beliefs, and everyone holds space for one another's healing. The Weekly Witch's Recovery Circle is not just a meeting; it's a ritual gathering of support, connection, and Magickal transformation.

Each week, witches in recovery come together to share their experiences, process challenges, and celebrate victories, big and small. The circle is guided by tarot, intuition, and spiritual discussion, allowing each participant to tune into their inner wisdom while feeling held by the collective energy of the group.

For many witches, recovery can feel isolating. Traditional recovery meetings often lack the spiritual connection that we crave. This circle bridges the gap, offering both practical recovery support and deep spiritual nourishment. It's a place to be reminded of your power, to set intentions, and to work through any blocks that may be holding you back. Over time, attending these weekly circles becomes more than just a support system—it becomes a sacred ritual that keeps you grounded in your recovery and your Magick.

The Monthly Deep Dive into the Witch's Tools for Recovery

Recovery is a journey, and like any journey, it requires tools to navigate it successfully. The Monthly Deep Dive into the Witch's Tools for Recovery is an opportunity to explore those tools in a structured yet Magickal way. Each month, we take a focused look at one aspect of witchcraft that can support your sobriety, whether it's divination, protection Magick, shadow work, or energy clearing.

These sessions are interactive and exploratory, designed for witches who are ready to integrate spiritual practices into their recovery journey. Unlike traditional classes, these deep dives allow participants to actively engage—asking questions, experimenting with techniques, and sharing insights as they unfold.

Picture yourself in a space where you are not just learning, but experiencing—casting protection spells to shield yourself from negativity, using tarot spreads to gain clarity on your emotional triggers, or working through a ritual to release shame and guilt from the past. The goal of these deep dives is to help you build a personalized, Magickal toolkit that supports your ongoing recovery. Over time, these tools become second nature, woven into the fabric of your daily life, helping you stay aligned, empowered, and in tune with your higher self.

The Quarterly Sober Witch Activation Workshop

Sometimes, we need more than just ongoing support—we need a breakthrough experience. That's what the Quarterly Sober Witch Activation Workshop is all about. This three-hour immersive experience is designed to awaken your personal power, activate your Magickal potential, and solidify your recovery path through deep, intentional work.

During this workshop, you will be guided through a series of rituals, energy practices, and hands-on Magickal work designed to help you claim your identity as a Sober Witch. One of the most profound aspects of this workshop is the creation of your own Recovery Staff—a sacred tool that serves as a symbol of your journey, your strength, and your commitment to both your sobriety and your spirituality.

The experience of crafting this staff is transformational. It is more than just assembling an object—it is infusing your energy, your intentions, and your Magick into a tool that will walk with you throughout your recovery. This workshop is a moment of empowerment, healing, and self-affirmation, one that stays with you long after the session has ended.

For many witches, this workshop is a turning point—a shift from feeling like they are simply "getting by" in recovery to truly owning their power and stepping into their highest self.

Illuminate: The Unschool of Sober Witchcraft

Recovery is not a one-size-fits-all journey, and neither is spiritual growth. Illuminate: The Unschool of Sober Witchcraft was created to allow witches in recovery to learn at their own pace, explore their spirituality on their own terms, and dive deep into teachings that resonate with them.

This digital learning space offers courses, workbooks, and rituals that support both sobriety and Magickal practice. Whether you want to strengthen your intuition, deepen your understanding of energy work, or learn practical spellcraft for emotional healing, Illuminate offers the space to do so in a way that is accessible and self-directed.

Imagine sitting with a journal, working through shadow work prompts that help you uncover and release limiting beliefs. Picture yourself studying the cycles of the moon, learning how to align your recovery milestones with lunar phases. Envision casting spells that reinforce your commitment to yourself, your healing, and your growth.

The beauty of Illuminate is that it allows you to move at your own pace. There are no deadlines, no pressure—just knowledge, inspiration, and guidance to help you evolve as both a sober individual and a practicing witch.

The Recovery Coven Membership

Recovery is not just about abstaining from substances—it's about building a life that feels Magickal, fulfilling, and deeply aligned with who you are. The Recovery Coven is a space where you can do just that, surrounded by others who uplift and support you.

At the heart of all these resources lies The Recovery Coven, a community of witches who are walking this path together. This membership is more than just a collection of courses and workshops—it is an ongoing support system, a sacred space, and a circle of connection.

What's Included in The Recovery Coven Membership?

- **The Course Library: Magick for Empowered Living** – A growing collection of courses and digital products designed to support both your sobriety and spiritual journey, including:
  - Protection Magick
  - Binaural Beat Affirmations
  - Alchemy of Recovery
  - 90 Days of Shadow Work
  - ## Grimoire of Recovery

- **Live Monthly Workshops and Ritual Circles** – Engage in interactive and transformative sessions designed to keep you aligned with your Magickal path and grounded in sobriety:
  - Full Moon Gratitude Ritual
  - New Moon Intention Ritual

- The Claires Psychic Development Workshop
- Psychic Hot Seat Workshop
- Self-Care for Witches
- Spellcraft Workshops
- Creative Alchemy for Recovery

- **24/7 Access to The Recovery Coven Community** (via the Sober Witch Life App) – A private space where you can connect, ask questions, share your journey, and receive ongoing support from other witches in recovery, available anytime, day or night.

The Recovery Coven provides access to everything mentioned above, plus it's a place where you can ask questions, seek support, share your wins, and receive encouragement from witches who understand your journey.

One of the most powerful aspects of The Recovery Coven is its annual in-person retreat—a time for witches in recovery to come together, step away from their everyday lives, and immerse themselves in healing, ritual, and spiritual connection. Imagine gathering under the stars, engaging in sacred ceremonies, deep discussions, and transformative experiences that remind you just how powerful you truly are.

Recovery is not just about abstaining from substances—it's about building a life that feels Magickal, fulfilling, and deeply aligned with who you are. The Recovery Coven is a space where you can do just that, surrounded by others who uplift and support you.

A Personal Note from Me

I created these resources because I know what it feels like to long for guidance that truly resonates. When I first stepped into recovery, I found myself searching for tools that spoke to my spirit as much as they supported my sobriety. It became clear to me that there was a need for a space where witches in recovery could feel at home—where they could heal in a way that honored both their Magick and their personal transformation. That is why I poured my heart into building these resources, ensuring that no witch ever has to feel like they are walking this path alone.

It is my greatest honor to hold space for you, to offer these tools, and to walk this journey beside you. Being able to support witches in recovery is not just something I do—it is **part of my life's purpose**, and I feel truly blessed to share this work. Whether you are just beginning or have been on this path for years, I want you to know that **you are seen, you are valued, and you are never alone**.

May your recovery be filled with **Magick, empowerment, and the unwavering knowledge that you are capable of incredible transformation**.

With love, light, and eternal gratitude,

Sunshine ☐

MAGICKTAILS: SPIRIT FREE, INTENTION HEAVY

A Magick potion, crafted by a witch's own hands and infused with pure intention, holds more power than any store-bought or man-made spirit, for it carries the soul's essence in every drop.

Or, as I also like to call them, potions. Because, well, I'm always trying to put Magick into every little thing that I do. So for me, crafting a wickedly delicious, non-alcoholic drink is more than mixing ingredients—it's infusing intention, energy, and kitchen Magick into a sip of something truly special.

But why choose these Magickal potions over a traditional alcoholic beverage? The answer lies in a shift many of us are craving, whether consciously or not. In a world where alcohol is stitched into almost every social fabric—from celebrations to casual dinners—it can be challenging to navigate situations without the pull of a drink. It's in toasts, holiday traditions, and even self-care rituals, where a glass of wine has somehow become synonymous with unwinding. For some, this ingrained culture can feel restrictive, isolating, or even triggering.

Creating and enjoying alcohol-free, Magick-infused drinks isn't just about having a substitute. It's about reclaiming rituals and creating new ones that align with our well-being and personal power. When we choose to blend herbs, fruits, and intention in our own potions, we're shifting the focus from mindless indulgence to mindful connection. We're choosing self-care that nourishes us without the hangover—both literal and emotional.

These drinks serve as reminders that we can celebrate, relax, and honor moments without needing to dim our consciousness or step outside our authentic selves. They are gateways to pleasure and presence, where Magick isn't an afterthought but a main ingredient. This way, every sip is a spell, every flavor is a note in a harmonious brew, and every glass is an invitation to indulge in joy and ceremony that uplifts the spirit.

So, why not raise a glass, filled to the brim with Magick and intention, and toast to a life where every ritual can be savored fully—alcohol-free?

❋ ❋ ❋

Lucid Mulled Cider

This is a delicious beverage for the fall. It is one that I will brew for Samhain and then put any leftovers in the fridge and reheat for a few weeks after. It's wonderful for dream work or when you are looking to explore the astral plane.

Supplies
- 1 Gallon Cider
- 1 cup of fresh or frozen cranberries
- 1 large naval orange sliced
- 2 cinnamon sticks
- 1 tsp whole allspice
- 1 tsp whole cloves
- ½ tsp black pepper corn
- 3 to 5 tbsp of dried mugwort

- 1 to 5 tbsp of dried catmint
- Cheese cloth or clean nylon stocking
- Caldron, crockpot or large pot

Directions

1. Add the cider, cranberries and the sliced orange into whatever vessel you choose to cook/warm the drink in.
2. Put the spices and herbs into the cheese cloth (layered) or the nylon stocking. (Yes I will use nylons that I've run in hot water only)
3. Toss your Magick "tea bag" into the vessel
   a. If on the stove - bring to a boil and then reduce it to a simmer, allowing it to simmer for 30 minutes to an hour.
   b. If in a crock pot - put it on low and allow it to cook for 4 hours.
4. When done, remove the Magick tea bag and toss it.

Serving

Keep in mind that mugwort is bitter so this will not be as sweet as a drink as the cider starts out as. Serve it warm and garnish with an orange slice and a cinnamon stick. If you'd like it a little sweeter, add a bit of local honey. Consume this around 1 to 2 hours before you want to drift to sleep or attempt to astral project.

All We Need is Love Potion

I often have this incredibly strong concoction on hand in the house. I use it when I have a new friend over to help and strengthen the love between us. It is SUPER strong and concentrated so I will always add it to something else.

Supplies

- 4 cups of dried hibiscus flowers
- 1 cup of dried lemongrass
- 1 gallon mason jar

- Water to fill the jar
- 1 Cup of honey

Directions

1. Place the dried ingredients in the mason jar and cover it with water. Screw on the lid and place it in the fridge
2. Allow it to sit in the fridge for 16 to 24 hours
3. Strain the liquid out and put it into another mason jar
4. Add the one cup of honey, put the lid on and shake it to mix
5. While you're shaking it state, "May this potion be infused with sweetness, kindness and compassion. May all that share in this potion, share in divine love.
6. Keep refrigerated

Serving

This potion would be super concentrated. I strongly recommend adding it into some sparkling water over ice or even a lemon lime soda if you'd like something sweeter. Share this beverage with someone you want to form a loving relationship with.

Another "mimosa" style - mix it with orange juice and tonic water to serve it with Sunday brunch.

Passion Punch

Once upon a time every first date started with an alcoholic beverage. Yes it lowered inhibitions, but it could also make this a little bit more challenging too. I did miss that ritual of enjoying a drink with a lover so I created this little delightful mix to help kick the night up a notch.

Supplies

- 4 oz of hot water
- ½ oz of dried damiana leaf
- 8 oz of pineapple juice
- 4 to 6 ripe strawberries with greenery removed
- 2 tablespoons of honey

Directions

1. Steep the damiana leaf in the 4 oz of hot water for 15 to 20 minutes and then strain. Add the honey so that it dissolves and allow it to cool.
2. Add the pineapple juice and muddle the strawberries in the beverage
3. Serve it in two glasses over ice

Serving

You could easily double this recipe if you'd like two glasses. I've found that I don't always even finish one glass before I can't keep my hands off my partner. I'd also recommend adding some more tropical fruit juices to change up the taste profile or even leave the honey out if you don't like it that sweet.

Moonlit Mango Elixir

Friendship dates once had the spellbinding charm of a shared drink under the stars. While alcohol used to be the go-to for such occasions, this enchanting, non-alcoholic creation offers the same magic without the blur. Sip, savor, and let the night bewitch you.

Supplies

- 4 oz of hot water
- ½ oz of dried hibiscus flowers
- 8 oz of mango nectar
- 1 lime, cut into wedges
- 1 tablespoon of agave syrup or maple syrup (optional)
- A sprig of fresh mint for garnish

Directions

1. Steep the hibiscus flowers in the hot water for 15 to 20 minutes, then strain. Stir in the agave syrup (or maple syrup) while still warm to dissolve it, then let the

infusion cool.

2. Add the mango nectar to the hibiscus mixture.
3. Squeeze the juice from a few lime wedges into the drink and gently muddle them for a tangy twist.
4. Serve over ice in two glasses, and top each with a sprig of fresh mint.

Serving

This recipe makes two glasses perfect for sharing, but you can easily double it if desired. Enjoy it as is, or feel free to add a splash of sparkling water for a fizzy kick. Before you know it, the rich, floral, and fruity notes will have you giggling and laughing while your evening unfolding with sweet adventure.

Tranquil Flower Brew

Inspired by the rituals of unwinding and the power of nature's gifts, this recipe is designed for those who seek deep relaxation and calm without a drop of alcohol. Perfect for winding down after a long day or when you need a soothing moment during a busy season.

Supplies

- 2 tablespoons of chamomile flowers
- 1 tablespoon of lemon balm
- 18 oz of water
- 1 teaspoon of ashwagandha root
- 1 tablespoon of maple syrup (or sweetener of choice)

Directions

1. Steep the chamomile flowers and lemon balm in 8 oz of hot water for 20 minutes. For a stronger brew, let it infuse overnight.
2. In a separate pot, boil the ashwagandha root in the remaining 8 oz of water for 20 minutes.
3. Strain both infusions and combine them in a teapot or serving vessel.

4. Stir in the maple syrup for a touch of natural sweetness.
5. Serve warm and enjoy.

Serving

This brew makes about four servings. It can be sipped immediately for instant tranquility or stored in the refrigerator and reheated when needed. Perfect for cozy evenings or moments when you need a gentle, herbal embrace to ease your mind.

Mindful Citrus Tonic

In a world buzzing with distractions, finding clarity and focus can feel elusive. This invigorating drink, infused with natural boosters, is your secret weapon for sharpening the mind and steadying the spirit. Sip and reclaim your focus.

Supplies

- 4 oz of hot water
- 1 teaspoon of dried calamus root
- 1 teaspoon of rosemary
- 8 oz of freshly squeezed orange juice
- 1 teaspoon of matcha powder
- 1 tablespoon of lemon juice
- 1 tablespoon of honey (optional)
- Orange slices and rosemary sprigs for garnish

Directions

1. Steep the dried rosemary and calamus root in hot water for 10 to 15 minutes, then strain and let it cool.
2. In a separate container, dissolve the matcha powder in a small amount of warm water until smooth.
3. Combine the rosemary infusion, orange juice, matcha mixture, and lemon juice in a large glass or pitcher. Stir well.
4. Add honey if you prefer a touch of sweetness.

5. Serve over ice and garnish with orange slices and a rosemary sprig for an aromatic finish.

Serving

This tonic serves two glasses, perfect for a morning focus session or an afternoon pick-me-up. The earthy notes of the calamus root, rosemary and matcha blend seamlessly with the bright citrus flavors, creating a refreshing drink that sharpens the senses and supports mental clarity. For an extra twist, try adding a splash of sparkling water for a light, effervescent finish.

Peace Sweet Tea

Perfect for friendly gatherings and moments when you wish to infuse peace into your circle, this peach-flavored sweet tea blends calming herbs and fruit for a delightful drink. Sip and share this tea as a token of peace and warmth.

Supplies

- 2 ripe peaches, sliced
- 1 tablespoon of dried chamomile flowers
- 1 tablespoon of black tea
- 1 teaspoon of dried hibiscus petals (for color and subtle tang)
- 16 oz of water
- 2 tablespoons of honey (or sweetener of your choice)
- Fresh mint leaves for garnish

Directions

1. In a pot, bring the water to a gentle boil. Add the chamomile flowers and hibiscus petals, allowing them to steep for 15 to 20 minutes.
2. While the infusion is steeping, place the sliced peaches in a bowl and gently muddle them to release their natural juices.

3. Strain the herbal infusion and pour it over the muddled peaches. Let the mixture sit for 10 minutes to blend the flavors.
4. Strain the tea again to remove peach pieces and herbal residue. Stir in the honey until fully dissolved.
5. Chill the tea in the refrigerator or serve over ice with fresh mint leaves as garnish.

Serving

This recipe makes about four servings and can easily be doubled or tripled for larger gatherings. "Peace Sweet Tea" is best enjoyed in good company, where every sip is a reminder of friendship, harmony, and moments of shared tranquility.

MAGICKAL GLOSSARY

I'm including this Magickal glossary to ensure that readers, whether seasoned practitioners or newcomers to witchcraft and recovery, have a clear understanding of the terms and practices woven throughout this book. The journey of recovery, especially when intertwined with Magick, can involve unique concepts and language that may be unfamiliar or open to interpretation. This glossary serves as a guiding light, offering insight and clarity into these essential terms so that you can fully embrace the wisdom, rituals, and tools shared within these pages. My hope is that it deepens your connection to your own path and enriches your experience with each step.

Affirmation: A positive statement used to challenge and overcome negative or unhelpful thoughts. Often repeated daily to instill confidence or manifest goals.

Al-Anon: A support group for friends and family members of alcoholics, providing a space to share experiences and support each other through the challenges of having a loved one with addiction.

Amends: The process of acknowledging and taking responsibility for past actions that have harmed others. In this book, making amends is a part of the Magickal journey to heal relationships and restore balance.

Ancestor Work: The practice of connecting with one's ancestors for guidance, healing, and support. In this book, ancestor work is emphasized as a source of strength and wisdom during the recovery journey.

Astral Projection: The practice of separating one's consciousness from the physical body to explore the astral plane, often experienced during deep meditation or sleep.

Binding Spell: A type of spell used to restrict or prevent someone or something from causing harm or influencing negatively. Often used for protection.

Book of Shadows: A personal journal used by witches to record spells, rituals, reflections, and learnings. In the context of this book, it serves as a sacred space for documenting the recovery journey and Magickal practices.

Chakra: Energy centers within the body that are believed to regulate different aspects of physical, emotional, and spiritual well-being. There are seven main chakras, each associated with a specific area of the body and different emotions or qualities.

Chakra Work: Practices focused on aligning the seven chakras to improve physical, emotional, and spiritual well-being. Techniques include meditation, visualization, and using crystals or essential oils.

Cleansing: The act of removing negative energy from an object, space, or person, often using tools like sage, palo santo, or incense.

Codependency: A behavioral condition where someone excessively relies on another person for validation, self-esteem, or emotional stability, often compromising their own needs. In this book, codependency is explored in the context of past relationships and how it affects personal recovery.

Correspondences: Specific associations between objects (like herbs, crystals, colors) and their Magickal properties. Used in spells and rituals to amplify desired effects.

Courage Spell: A ritual or set of actions designed to invoke bravery and strength in oneself or others.

Coven: A supportive community of witches who come together for rituals, sharing, and collective Magickal work. In this book, the coven represents the power of community in the recovery process.

Daily Recovery Circle: A gathering, either in person or virtual, where witches in recovery come together to share their experiences, offer support, and strengthen their connection to the community. These circles are vital for maintaining accountability and emotional well-being.

Divination: The practice of seeking knowledge of the future or the unknown through spiritual means, such as Tarot, runes, or pendulums. Divination tools help witches in recovery gain insight and guidance.

Energy Vibration: The frequency at which one's energy is said to vibrate, reflecting their emotional and spiritual state. Higher vibrations are associated with positive states like love and peace.

Empath: A person who can sense and often absorb the emotions and energies of others. Empaths are typically highly sensitive and may require practices to protect their energy.

Full Moon Release Ritual: A ritual performed during the full moon to release negative energies or old habits that no longer serve one's highest good. The ritual often involves writing down what is to be released and burning the paper under the moonlight.

Grounding: A practice used to connect oneself to the present moment and the earth's energy. Grounding techniques are often employed to stay centered, especially during moments of stress or emotional upheaval in recovery.

Grounding Tool: Objects or actions used to reconnect with the earth's energy and stabilize emotions or thoughts. Examples include grounding stones like hematite or black tourmaline, or physical practices like yoga.

Guided Meditation: A form of meditation led by an instructor or recording, guiding the practitioner through visualization or relaxation techniques.

Herbal Infusion: A drink made by steeping herbs in water, often used for their Magickal or medicinal properties.

Higher Powers: A term used to describe spiritual forces greater than oneself, including deities, ancestors, spirit guides, or the Universe. In this book, the concept encourages reliance on these forces to aid in recovery and spiritual growth.

Invocation: The act of calling upon a deity, spirit, or higher power for assistance or guidance. Invocations are a key part of rituals and spellwork in this book, helping to draw in supportive energies.

Invocation for Courage: A prayer or ritual used to call upon spiritual entities for the courage needed to face challenges in recovery. This is often done during specific lunar phases or in moments of emotional difficulty.

Intention: A focused goal or desire set before performing Magick or rituals. Intentions are the driving force behind spells and are crucial for manifesting change during the recovery process.

Journaling Prompts: Specific questions or statements used to guide reflective writing, helping one explore emotions, memories, and triggers deeply. Journaling is emphasized in this book as a tool for emotional processing and shadow work.

Magick: The art of using one's will, intention, and energy to create change in oneself or the world around them. Different from stage magic or illusion, Magick involves ritual, spells, and focused energy work. In this book, Magick is seen as a tool to empower the recovery process.

Manifestation: The practice of bringing something into reality through focused intention and energy work. Often involves visualization and affirmations.

Mugwort: An herb commonly used in Magick and dream work. Known for its protective and visionary properties.

New Moon: The lunar phase when the moon is invisible from Earth, symbolizing new beginnings and the perfect time for setting intentions.

New Moon Ritual: A ritual performed during the new moon

phase, focused on setting intentions for new beginnings. In the context of recovery, this ritual is used to release old habits and welcome new, healthier patterns.

Personification: The practice of giving human characteristics to non-human entities, such as referring to addiction as a 'drinking demon' in ritual work.

Recovery Intention Ritual: A ritual designed specifically to set intentions around one's recovery journey, often performed during significant lunar phases or personal milestones to reinforce commitment and focus.

Ritual: A series of actions performed in a set order to achieve a specific outcome, often with spiritual or Magickal significance. Can be simple or elaborate, depending on the intention. Rituals are used throughout the recovery process to mark milestones and support personal transformation.

Ritual Bath: A cleansing ritual involving a bath infused with herbs, oils, or crystals, used to prepare oneself spiritually before performing Magick or spellwork. It is a way to cleanse energy and focus intentions.

Salt Bath: A ritual bath using salts like Epsom or sea salt, combined with essential oils, to cleanse and ground oneself energetically. Salt baths are used to wash away negative energies and restore balance.

Samhain: A pagan festival marking the end of the harvest season, celebrated on October 31st. It is a time when the veil between the physical and spiritual worlds is believed to be thinnest.

Shadow Work: The practice of exploring and integrating the hidden or repressed parts of oneself. Often involves self-reflection, journaling, and meditation to understand and heal past traumas or negative patterns. It is an integral part of the recovery process, allowing for healing and growth.

Sober Witch: An individual who identifies as a witch and is committed to a path of sobriety, using Magick and spiritual practices to support their recovery and personal growth.

Spell: A set of words, actions, and objects used in ritual to manifest a specific outcome. Often involves correspondences such as herbs, crystals, and candles.

Spellwork: The act of creating and performing spells to manifest specific outcomes. Spellwork in this book is used to support recovery goals, promote healing, and reinforce personal growth.

Sponsor: A mentor or guide who supports another person through their recovery journey, usually someone with more experience in sobriety. Sponsors offer emotional support, guidance, and accountability.

Tarot: A form of divination using a deck of cards to gain insights, guidance, and clarity. In this book, Tarot is used as a tool to connect with one's higher powers and support the recovery journey.

Tarot Spread: A specific arrangement of tarot cards used in divination to answer a question or gain insight into a situation. Each card's position has a different meaning, contributing to the overall interpretation.

Third Eye: The chakra associated with intuition and insight, located on the forehead between the eyes. It's believed to be the center of perception and spiritual awareness.

Third Step Prayer: A personalized prayer created by the individual to surrender control and ask for guidance from higher powers. This prayer helps maintain spiritual alignment and serves as a daily practice for staying grounded in recovery.

ABOUT THE AUTHOR

Sunshine Witchski

Sunshine is a trailblazing Psychic Medium, Soul Healer, Spiritual Advisor, High Priestess, Reiki Master, and Recovering Alcoholic. Known as The Pink-haired Sober Witch, her mission is to help highly motivated witches in recovery rediscover their magick, align with their highest purpose, and live the abundant life promised in sobriety.

She is the visionary behind Illuminate: The Unschool of Sober Witchcraft, a revolutionary platform dedicated to supporting witches in recovery. This groundbreaking initiative includes the Sober Witch Life mobile app—the first of its kind—available on both iOS and Android. The app provides free, transformative resources like the Sober Witch's Tool Kit and weekly recovery circles. For those seeking deeper connection and growth, Sunshine created the Recovery Coven membership, offering exclusive workshops, rituals, and a supportive community to help witches stay grounded and empowered on their recovery journey.

Sunshine is also the host of two impactful podcasts: The Sober Witch Life, which focuses on recovery through magick and spiritual empowerment, and The Deepest Spirituality Podcast, which explores the transformative power of spiritual practices. Her expertise has made her a sought-after guest on podcasts across the globe, where she shares her insights on blending witchcraft with recovery and spiritual awakening.

In addition to her spiritual work, Sunshine is an award-winning software product manager and business operations expert who has helped major corporations reimagine their internal processes, cultivate innovation, and implement cutting-edge solutions that drive success.

When she's not mentoring witches in recovery or revolutionizing corporate systems, Sunshine finds joy in creative pursuits. She loves dancing, cooking, painting, and spending time with her niece, her partner, his kids, and their five adorable kitties at her home in the Detroit suburbs.

"Only when we know our own darkness can we sit in the darkness with others." - Pema Chodron

https://www.illuminateunschool.com
https://www.soberwitch.life
https://www.youtube.com/@IlluminateUnschoolofWitchcraft
https://www.facebook.com/groups/soberwitchsbazaar/
https://www.linkedin.com/in/jenromanowski/
https://www.facebook.com/jen.romanowski/

www.ingramcontent.com/pod-product-compliance
Lightning Source LLC
Chambersburg PA
CBHW061753120626
46550CB00005B/1983